GREAT PASSENGER SHIPS 1930–1940

WILLIAM H. MILLER

The History Press

Commissioned in 1936, the *Queen Mary* was the pride of the then huge British merchant navy. She was also a ship of distinction – alone, there were 600 clocks on board the 80,00grt super liner. (Cunard Line)

First published 2015

The History Press
The Mill, Brimscombe Port
Stroud, Gloucestershire, GL5 2QG
www.thehistorypress.co.uk

© William H. Miller, 2015

The right of William H. Miller to be identified as the Author of this work has been asserted in accordance with the Copyright, Designs and Patents Act 1988.

All rights reserved. No part of this book may be reprinted or reproduced or utilised in any form or by any electronic, mechanical or other means, now known or hereafter invented, including photocopying and recording, or in any information storage or retrieval system, without the permission in writing from the Publishers.

British Library Cataloguing in Publication Data.
A catalogue record for this book is available from the British Library.

ISBN 978 0 7509 6309 1

Typesetting and origination by The History Press
Printed in China

CONTENTS

	Foreword	5
	Acknowledgements	6
	Introduction	7
1.	Transatlantic: White Star and Two New Liners	9
2.	Bound for Shanghai: *Empress of Japan* (1930)	14
3.	Colonial Service: *Johan van Oldenbarnevelt* (1930)	17
4.	Might, Style and Splendour: *Empress of Britain* (1931)	21
5.	Long-Lasting Liner: *Monterey* (1932)	24
6.	Sailing Coastal: American 'Mini Liners'	27
7.	Italian Super Liner: *Conte di Savoia* (1932)	31
8.	The Honeymoon Ship: *Queen of Bermuda* (1933)	34
9.	Thirties Dreamboats: *Normandie* (1935) and *Queen Mary* (1936)	37
10.	Spy Ship: *Batory* (1936)	46
11.	An Enduring German: *Pretoria* (1936)	69
12.	'Strength through Joy' and The World's First Large Cruise Ship	71
13.	Dutch Beauty: *Nieuw Amsterdam* (1938)	74
14.	Cruising to the Sun: Winter 1938–39	78
15.	The 'Sunshine Ship': *Mauretania* (1939)	81

16.	Luxury to South America: *Andes* (1939)	84
17.	Tension and Uncertainty: The Summer of 1939	88
18.	The Southampton Docks: September 1939	93
	Bibliography	96

FOREWORD

I have many of Bill Miller's books and they, especially in the photographs, have brought back many memories for me. As a boy in the 1930s, I used to ride the harbour ferries – to Hoboken, Jersey City and of course back and forth to Staten Island – just to watch passenger ships, both large and small. I recall seeing the *Île de France*, *Kungsholm*, *Vulcania*, *Samaria* and the little *Noordam* sail past – like a convoy with one ship after another – on a Saturday morning. I also recall seeing the *Britannic* as she broke through the fog of a November day, the *Santa Rosa* and other Grace liners departing on Fridays and the joy of seeing either the *Monarch of Bermuda* or *Queen of Bermuda* speeding off on a Saturday afternoon.

Of course, the greatest treat was to visit the West Side piers. As a little boy watching, I could stand before each liner – and sometimes even go aboard. I remember one occasion when the *Normandie*, *Aquitania*, *Rex* and *Bremen* were in port together. What a collection of great ships! Then, with waving passengers on deck and clouds of white smoke from their thunderous whistles and as tugs pushed and pulled, they sailed off – one by one until the piers were all but empty.

This book, Bill Miller's latest, promises to bring back more memories for me. Happily, he keeps the subject of the great ocean liners alive!

Robert Gordon
New York City, 2015

ACKNOWLEDGEMENTS

It takes many hands to create a book such as this – gathering photos, anecdotes, tales from long-ago ships and their voyages. As author, I am much like the chief purser – organising everything. Many kind thanks are therefore due, of course. First, appreciation to The History Press and Amy Rigg for taking this project on and adding to the series. Very special thanks also to Stephen Card for his brilliant covers, to Robert Gordon for his Foreword and to Michael Hadgis for his technical assistance.

First-class thanks also to the late Frank Cronican, Maurizio Eliseo, Richard Faber, John Ferguson, the late John Gillespie, the late John Havers, Pine Hodges, the late Andrew Kilk, Norman Knebel, Anthony La Forgia, Anton Logvinenko, Ian Robertson, Don Stoltenberg, the late Everett Viez, Richard Weiss and Albert Wilhelmi. And a round of thanks to other assistants and contributors: the late J.K. Byass, Robert Cummings, Gordon Dalzell, the late Alex Duncan, Billie Ellis, John Draffin, the late Rupert Ferguson, Peter Knego, the late Vincent Messina, Jeanette Moran, Captain George Panagiotakis, Paolo Piccione, Selim San, the late Roger Scozzafava and Roger Sherlock.

Companies and organisations that deserve a nod of special thanks include Crystal Cruises, Cunard Line, British India Line, Canadian Pacific Steamships, Chandris Cruises, Clipper Line, Flying Camera Inc., French Line, Hapag-Lloyd, Holland America Line, Italian Line, Matson Line, Moran Towing & Transportation Co., the National Railway Museum, Nedlloyd, the New York Herald Tribune, P&O, Port Authority of New York & New Jersey, RMS Foundation, Rotterdam Maritime Museum, Royal Mail Lines, Steamship Historical Society, World Ocean & Cruise Liner Society and World Ship Society.

William H. Miller, 2015

INTRODUCTION

Whilst the 1930s was a time of the worldwide Depression and the rise of sinister, militaristic regimes, it was also a time of great creativity – the likes of Hollywood films, soaring skyscrapers and, of course, many great ocean liners. These included some of the largest, longest, fastest and finest liners of all time. France's *Normandie*, commissioned in 1935, has often been called the 'most extravagant' and 'best decorated' liner of all time. Then there were the decorative splendours of such liners as the *Conte di Savoia*, *Queen Mary* and *Nieuw Amsterdam*.

In creating this book, for our series about decades of liners, I had more than enough ships to choose from, but finally narrowed the list. Historically, I began with the Depression and its early effects, namely the decline in transatlantic passengers and the gradual withering of the once great White Star Line, and finished with recollections of the Southampton Docks in the first, dark days of the Second World War. The careers of ships are, I feel, fascinating – they are like characters in a long novel – and altogether fit within the scope of historic events. Some readers will miss, even object, to the exclusion of their preferred, even favourite liners, but I decided to develop a varied range – from ship histories to the 'very real' rivalry between the *Normandie* and *Queen Mary* to cruising (including the Nazi 'Strength through Joy' concept) to memories of the New York City waterfront just as war in Europe was starting.

The '30s were indeed productive, and while I cannot mention all liners, herein is something of an overview. Just about every maritime nation was involved – and usually adding new ships. The Dutch, for example, built their biggest and finest liners yet for the colonial trade out to the East Indies – the sisters *Johan van Oldenbarnevelt* and *Marnix van St Aldegonde*, as well as the *Boleran* and *Dempo*. Similarly for colonial service, France's Messageries Maritimes created a string of liners that included the squat-stacked *Felix Roussel*, completed in 1930 and then not scrapped for forty-four years, in 1974. Canadian Pacific Steamships jumped forward with stunning, new flagships: the *Empress of Japan* for the Pacific and the even larger *Empress of Britain* on the Atlantic. Also for Pacific services, the Americans were busy – two liners, the 21,900-ton *President Hoover* and *President Coolidge*, and then a long-lasting trio for the Matson Line – the *Mariposa*, *Monterey* and *Lurline*. The United States Lines was interested in the Atlantic, however, and they added the biggest US-built liners yet, the 24,000-ton sisters *Washington* and *Manhattan*.

The French added to their Atlantic presence as well, but with two intermediate liners, the 25,000-ton *Lafayette* and 28,000-ton *Champlain*.

On the South Atlantic and in the wake of the decoratively innovative *Île de France* of 1927, France's Compagnie Sud-Atlantique introduced the lavish, if ill-fated, *L'Atlantique*. An art deco dreamboat, she was otherwise a very tragic ship – being destroyed by fire when only sixteen months old. For a far less lengthy service, the British added two splendid liners, the three-funnel *Monarch of Bermuda* and *Queen of Bermuda*.

Rather expectedly, British shipyards were very busy – P&O added no less than five Strath liners for its primary UK–Australia run: *Strathnaver*, *Strathaird*, *Strathmore*, *Stratheden* and *Strathallan*. The historic line also created, but for its alternate services to the Far East, the likes of the *Carthage*, *Corfu* and *Canton*. The rival Orient Line commissioned the decoratively important *Orion* and *Orcades*. Union-Castle was exceptionally ambitious and added no less than seven liners in just four years, between 1935 and 1939 – beginning with the speedy, 25,500-ton pair of *Stirling Castle* and *Athlone Castle*, then the larger *Capetown Castle* and then the sisters *Dunvegan Castle* & *Dunnottar Castle*, *Durban Castle* & *Pretoria Castle*. Even if White Star Line was winding down and long before its merger in 1934, with Cunard, it added the big, 27,000-ton motor liners *Britannic* and *Georgic*. Between the mighty *Queen Mary* and the expected *Queen Elizabeth*, officially due in the spring of 1940, Cunard added the *Mauretania*, a very handsome 35,000-tonner, which first appeared in that fateful summer of 1939. Other British ship owners also added new flagships – the *Dominion Monarch* for Shaw Savill Lines and the *Andes* for Royal Mail Lines.

The Germans looked to Eastern waters with three big, passenger-cargo combination ships: the 18,000-ton *Scharnhorst*, *Gneisenau* and *Potsdam*. They also added the twin-funnel *Windhuk* and *Pretoria* for African sailings. Then Hamburg shipbuilders produced the world's first large, 'pure and purposeful' cruise ships – the 1,465-passenger *Wilhelm Gustloff* and *Robert Ley* – for the Third Reich's 'Strength through Joy' programme.

The Italians all but outdid themselves with the giant *Rex* and sumptuous *Conte di Savoia*, but also added the speedy *Victoria* for service out to the Far East and two motor ships, the *Oceania* and *Neptunia*, for added services to South America.

The Dutch produced yet more liners, indeed some of their very finest ships – the splendid *Nieuw Amsterdam* for the North Atlantic and the *Oranje* for colonial sailings out East. They also added four of the finest, if smaller, combination passenger-cargo liners – the all-first-class *Noordam*, *Zaandam*, *Westerdam* and *Zuiderdam*. There was also a fine trio – the *Boissevain*, *Tegelberg* and *Ruys* – the biggest and finest yet for the distant South Africa–Far East run.

Out in Japan, the NYK Line was planning three big combo liners – the 250-passenger *Nitta Maru*, *Yawata Maru* and *Kasuga Maru* were being readied, starting in 1939, for added service to San Francisco. The OSK Line, with interests in the Japan–South America trade, added two new sisters – the 12,700-ton *Argentina Maru* and *Brazil Maru*.

The Poles jumped forward with two new Atlantic liners, the *Pilsudski* and *Batory*, and later a pair for South American sailings, the *Sobieski* and *Chrobry*, while Norway added a sparkling new flagship, the *Oslofjord*, and Sweden ordered the 28,000-ton *Stockholm*.

The high water, perhaps the zenith, of the 1930s came in 1935–36 with the completion of the brilliant *Normandie* and the illustrious *Queen Mary*. They were two of the finest – and most interesting and colourful – super liners ever to sail. Of course, in her continuing retirement in southern California as a floating hotel and museum, the *Queen Mary* lives on as a glorious link to this era.

This golden age of 1930s ocean liners concluded, in some ways, with the mighty *Queen Elizabeth* and the new flagship of the American fleet, the *America*. War suddenly started on 3 September 1939 and almost all passenger ship services were disrupted. The incomplete *Queen Elizabeth* did not have a celebratory maiden crossing, but instead made a secret dash to the safety of neutral New York; the *America*, unable to sail on her intended European voyages, was temporarily pressed into alternative cruise service on still safe Caribbean and trans-Panama Canal itineraries. Most sadly, in the years ahead, through to 1945, almost half of the world's ocean liners would be destroyed.

But now, in a far happier vein, this book is intended to be a review of a golden era – some of the great liners of the 1930s. It might even include a touch of vivid imagination: it might be 1935, at New York and the *Normandie* is sailing!

William H. Miller
Secaucus, New Jersey, 2015

1

TRANSATLANTIC: WHITE STAR AND TWO NEW LINERS

The general picture for passenger ship lines changed considerably after the dramatic Wall Street Crash of October 1929. Business changed drastically. On the Atlantic run, 1 million passengers crossed in 1930; within five years, by 1935, it had dropped by fifty per cent – to 500,000. Everyone it seemed was affected.

Britain's White Star Line was a prime example. A long-time competitor to Cunard, they were planning their biggest liner yet, the three-funnel, 60,000-ton *Oceanic* when the Crash occurred. Ordered from their preferred Harland & Wolff yard at Belfast, prior uncertainties in White Star's operation were soon increased. Prospects were not good. Quickly, the *Oceanic* project was cancelled and the first steel for that super liner went to a more moderate, more economically viable project – to the 27,000-ton *Britannic*. A sister, the *Georgic*, was planned as well.

The 712ft-long *Britannic* was commissioned in June 1930. The brightness and cheer of her introduction was dimmed somewhat by the gathering dark clouds of the Depression. Like so many others, the *Britannic* would have to struggle to fill all her berths in the ensuing years. In rather sleek, art deco moderne, she was a long and low ship – 'very motorship', as the late maritime historian Frank Braynard called her – with two squat stacks (only the second one actually worked; the forward one was the radio room), a raked bow and a classic cruiser stern. Danish-built Burmeister & Wain diesels were connected to her twin propellers. Passenger berths totalled 1,553 in three classes and there was room for cargo in no less than seven holds. Her transatlantic crossings were coupled with periodic Caribbean as well as Mediterranean cruises. She also ran a number of three-night weekend trips up to Halifax from New York. Fares for these started at $45 and proved popular as escapist, if short, jaunts away from the worries and stresses of the ongoing Depression. The *Britannic* was called to far more serious duty as the Second World War started in the late summer of 1939. She was painted over in grey and spent more than the next six years as a troop transport.

The *Georgic* first arrived exactly two years later, in June 1932. Made over as a trooper for wartime service, she was badly damaged in a Nazi air attack at Port Tewfik in Egypt on 14 July 1941. She burned furiously and was all but destroyed, but then later beached.

The late John Havers spent much of his life watching ships, especially the great liners, at Southampton. He went on to become a purser with the Union-Castle Line. Stationed at Port Suez early in the Second World War, he knew most ships – even if they were then painted in all-grey and had painted-out names. It was only by silhouette that identities might be possible. He recalled:

The 26,943grt *Britannic* arrives in Liverpool, being docked at the famed Princes Landing Stage. (Cunard Line)

10 GREAT PASSENGER SHIPS: 1930–1940

Busy afternoon: Although she was a ship of the 1930s, the *Britannic* endured until December 1960. By then she was the last liner of the original White Star fleet. In this view, dated September 1957, the 712ft-long *Britannic* is seen berthed at Pier 92, New York. Behind her from top to bottom are the *Independence*, *United States*, *Olympia*, *Flandre*, *Mauretania* and *Queen Mary*. It was a record day for New York Harbor – over 9,000 passengers were landed. (Port Authority of New York & New Jersey)

The troops aboard countless converted liners were transferred ashore by Nile ferries, all of which were piloted by turbaned Sudanese captains. These captains were proudest to serve the biggest ships. The *Aquitania*, as I well remember, seemed the most important to them with her four, tall funnels.

I especially recall the visit of the *Georgic* with lots of evacuees aboard. She was hit in a night raid. A bomb went down her elevator shaft. Fire started and then the air blowers blew the smoke throughout the ship. Crippled, burned and twisted, she was almost completely sunk – and thought to be beyond repair. Only her bow and stern were exposed. To most observers, she was finished. She was useless to the war effort. But with enormous persistence and staggering effort, she was salvaged and taken to Port Sudan, then Karachi and finally Bombay for gradual repairs. In January 1943, she began the long, very slow voyage home to Belfast for full repairs and rebuilding. To those of us who remembered and helped save her at Suez, we received a telegram at that time, 'I am doing 15 knots to Cape Town. Thank you and congratulations'.

In 1943, John Havers was sent home to Britain. He added, 'I came home in the *Britannic*, ironically the *Georgic*'s sister, from Port Suez to Liverpool via Augusta and Algiers. We travelled alongside the hospital ship *Frances Y. Slanger*, the former Italian liner *Saturnia*.'

Rebuilt with only one funnel and a forward mast, the *Georgic* returned to trooping just before the war ended, in December 1944. She was never the same again. 'Her decks were twisted and uneven,' said a former Cunard crew member. She was refitted in 1948, for 1,962 low-fare, one-class passengers only, and was operated by the Ministry of Transport for migrant services, mostly

Above: The 1930s were, in retrospect, something of a boom period for British ocean liners. P&O introduced five new Strath liners for its UK–Australia run including the 22,500grt *Strathnaver* and her sister *Straithaird*. The others were the *Strathmore*, *Stratheden* and *Strathallan*. (P&O)

Left: Morning sailings: Until the 1960s, summer days at New York were often the busiest for liners arriving or departing from Europe. In this view, dated 13 July 1956, the Greek Line's *New York* and the *Britannic* are already in mid-river, making 11:30 a.m. departures, and about to sail off; still at the piers are the *Flandre*, *Queen Elizabeth* and – but on the cruise run to Bermuda – the *Ocean Monarch*. (Port Authority of New York & New Jersey)

12 GREAT PASSENGER SHIPS: 1930–1940

Latin American sailings: For its Liverpool–Caribbean–Panama Canal–West Coast of South America run, Pacific Steam Navigation Co. – known as PNSC – added its largest, most luxurious liner yet, the 888-passenger *Reina Del Pacifico* in 1931. (Roger Sherlock)

between the UK and Australia, and also occasionally for peacetime trooping. Between 1950 and 1954, Cunard chartered the ship for budget summer season-only crossings, usually between Southampton, Le Havre, Halifax and New York. 'She was an unhappy ship. Cunard had troubles just to find a crew to staff her. She was rather crude in ways,' recalled a former steward. 'There were few tears when it was decided to retire the *Georgic*.' Just under 24 years old, she was delivered to scrappers at Faslane in the winter of 1956.

When the *Britannic* resumed Cunard-White Star service (the two great firms had merged in April 1934 for better security and efficiency in those Depression times) in May 1948, she actually retained her original White Star funnel colours of buff and black. Refurbished with an emphasis on post-war comfort, her quarters were restyled for 429 in first class and 569 in tourist. She crossed for most of the year between Liverpool, Cobh and New York. An annual Mediterranean–Black Sea cruise out of New York became a highlight. Minimum fares for these sixty-six-day voyages started at $1,275 in 1960. Rather unique to cruising, these cruises terminated at Southampton, but included return first-class passage to New York in any Cunarder including the *Queen Mary* and *Queen Elizabeth*.

In her 30th year, the *Britannic*'s end was advanced it seems. She had a massive mechanical breakdown in the spring of 1960, her posted sailings were cancelled and instead she remained at Pier 90 in Manhattan for months while undergoing thorough repairs. Using barges and floating derricks, it then ranked as the greatest pier-side repair job of its kind. It all cost Cunard

The British Government needed peacetime troop ships in the 1930s. The *Dunera* and her sister *Dilwara* were managed, however, by the British India Steam Navigation Company. They were commissioned in 1936–37. (British India)

TRANSATLANTIC: WHITE STAR AND TWO NEW LINERS

millions including bookings and cancellations. Altogether, as Atlantic liner passengers were declining at a staggering rate, Cunard managers decided to retire what was then the Company's oldest passenger ship. Months later, under a moody November sky, the *Britannic* sailed from New York for the very last time. After arriving at Liverpool, being de-stored and in the care of a reduced crew, the very last White Star liner sailed off to Inverkeithing in Scotland for breaking up. The handsome *Britannic* was finished: 1930–60.

Innovative decor: The 23,500grt *Orion* of the London-based Orient Line, completed in 1935, introduced sleek art deco interiors to the UK–Australia run. It was a style normally associated with the bigger, more famous Atlantic liners. (P&O)

Resembling a chic London night club, the charming First Class Café aboard the 20-knot *Orion*. (P&O)

Lighter tones: The First Class Gallery aboard the *Orion*, which carried 1,139 passengers divided as 486 in first class and 653 in tourist class. (P&O)

2

BOUND FOR SHANGHAI: *EMPRESS OF JAPAN* (1930)

'They had the finest fleet on the Pacific back in the 1920s – with their fine Empress liners: *Empress of Australia*, *Empress of Asia*, *Empress of Russia* and *Empress of Canada*,' recalled the late Everett Viez, an ardent ship enthusiast, traveller and one-time New York City-based travel agent:

> They offered a superb, exacting, multi-class service between Vancouver and Victoria and the Orient – to Honolulu, Yokohama, Kobe, Nagasaki, Shanghai, Hong Kong and Manila. The high spirits and increasing passenger loads of the second half of the '20s prompted a decision to build the biggest, best and fastest Canadian Pacific liner for Vancouver service. She went on to become one of the finest passenger ships of the twentieth century.

The 666ft-long *Empress of Japan* was built by one of the great shipbuilders of the day: Fairfield Shipbuilding and Engineering Co. Ltd of Glasgow. She was completed in the spring of 1930. Designed to be the fastest and most luxurious liner yet on the Vancouver–Far East service, she was bestowed with a regal-sounding name, honouring Imperial Japan. Emerging as a handsome ship, the new *Empress* was, in fact, a refined, slightly smaller version of the giant *Empress of Britain*, which was then still being built, and quite nearby, at the John Brown yard at Clydebank. The Pacific liner had a slightly more 'relaxed' profile with three evenly slanted funnels (the third was in fact a dummy). The big *Empress of Britain* was more imposing, mighty, even more majestic.

The *Empress of Japan* was richly appointed. Her decor strongly reflected the recent moderne, a style later dubbed art deco. It was not extreme, however, and did not preclude warmth and a sense of comfort. The public areas were made more pleasing to the eye, as well as inviting, by added touches: scattered soft chairs and long sofas, silk pillows, area carpets on highly polished floors, potted palms, stylised columns. The berthing was arranged in Pacific style: 399 in first class, 164 in second class, 100 third class and 510 in so-called Asiatic steerage (primarily for Asian migrants going eastward to Canada).

After completing an introductory Atlantic crossing to the St Lawrence, she then set sail – in the summer of 1930 – for Hong Kong via the Suez Canal. Arriving in Vancouver for the first time that August, she averaged a very respectable 21 knots on her first Pacific passage. In the following spring, on a run between Yokohama and Victoria, she averaged 22.27 knots. No ship on the Pacific could outpace her. Her record stood for thirty years, until the 1960s, when it was surpassed by an American freighter, the *Washington Mail*.

Queen of the Pacific: The *Empress of Japan* was the fastest liner on the trans-Pacific run in the 1930s. She was also a classically handsome three-funnel liner. (Roger Sherlock)

Aboard the *Empress of Japan*, it was five days from Vancouver to Honolulu, fourteen days to Yokohama, fifteen to Kobe, seventeen to Shanghai, twenty to Hong Kong and twenty-two days to Manila. First-class fares began at $125 between Vancouver and Honolulu, and from $85 in second class, $65 in third class and $50 in steerage. European servants could accompany first-class passengers for $110, Asian servants for $50. First-class fares all the way to Manila started at $343.

Following the outbreak of war in September 1939, Canadian Pacific's transpacific service was suspended and their liners called to duty and scattered. (This Pacific service would not be resumed after the Second World War, and instead Canadian Pacific concentrated on their North Atlantic operations.) The *Empress of Japan*, painted over in greys, was designated as a troopship and sent to the South Pacific to take part in at least two noted convoys. The first, in January 1940, included three columns of converted troopers: HMS *Kent* led the *Empress of Japan*, *Empress of Canada*, *Orcades* and *Rangitata*; the battleship HMS *Ramillies* led the *Orion*, *Orcades* and *Dunera*; and then the French warship *Suffren* led the *Strathaird*, *Strathnaver*, *Otranto* and *Sobieski*. In the following May, the *Empress of Japan* was part of one of the biggest convoys of the war, one that included the *Queen Mary*, *Aquitania*, *Empress of Britain*, *Mauretania*, *Andes* and *Empress of Canada*. The combined tonnages of these seven liners was over 277,000.

In October 1942, prompted by Japan's entry into the war, the *Empress of Japan* was given special Government permission to be renamed, becoming the *Empress of Scotland*. Ships could not be renamed during the war primarily for security reasons. Later used on the North Atlantic troop shuttle, she was not decommissioned and returned to Canadian Pacific until the fall of 1948. She had steamed over 500,000 miles during eight years of military service, made three around-the-world trips and carried over 200,000 personnel. Refitted at her builders at Glasgow, she was styled for transatlantic service – between Liverpool and Quebec City.

The refitted *Empress* now wore red and white chequers on her three funnels and had greatly reduced berthing figures – 458 in first class and 205 in tourist class. She joined two other pre-war liners, the *Empress of Canada* and *Empress of France*, in providing a weekly service in each direction. Fares aboard the *Empress of Scotland* were from $246 in first class and $156 in tourist class.

Her most distinguished passengers came aboard in November 1951. She carried Her Royal Highness Princess Elizabeth and the Duke of Edinburgh, and their party home from a highly successful North American tour (and similar to the one in May–June 1939 carried out by the Princess's parents, King George VI and Queen Elizabeth, and who crossed both ways by sea –

Empress of Japan farewell: Gala departure from Vancouver. (ALF Collection)

the *Empress of Australia* over, the *Empress of Britain* on the return). Princess Mary, the Princess Royal and Princess Alice, the Countess of Athlone, were among other royals that used Canadian Pacific liners during their travels. Princess Elizabeth and Prince Philip boarded from a specially arranged stop at Portugal Cove in Newfoundland and then disembarked six days later at Liverpool. The voyage was said to have had some 'very rough patches' – the Princess, it was later reported, did not miss a meal while the Duke, himself a naval officer, took to his bedroom at times. The royal train was waiting at Liverpool and then delivered the royal couple to London. Sadly, within two months, King George VI would be dead and the young Princess would become Queen Elizabeth II.

In winter, the *Empress of Scotland* crossed to New York each December and then began three or four months of cruising to the sunny Caribbean. She then became an all-first-class ship and had a portable pool fitted to her aft deck.

With the addition of the brand-new *Empress of Britain* and *Empress of England* in 1956–57, the *Empress of Scotland* was made redundant to Canadian Pacific's requirements by the fall of 1957. Together with the *Queen Mary*, they were by then the last Atlantic three-stackers (a third liner with three funnels, the *Queen of Bermuda*, was on the New York–Bermuda run).

16 GREAT PASSENGER SHIPS: 1930–1940

Laid up at Liverpool, the *Empress of Scotland* was 28 years old and might well have gone to the breakers, but good fortune prevailed. She was sold for £1 million to the West Germans, to the newly formed Hamburg Atlantic Line. Provisionally renamed *Scotland*, she was sent off to Hamburg.

Gutted and largely rebuilt and modernised, the former *Empress* was all but unrecognisable when she appeared on the Atlantic liner scene as the streamlined, twin-funnel *Hanseatic* in the following July. The passenger accommodation had been greatly enlarged – to eighty-five in club-like, upper-deck first class and 1,167 in very comfortable tourist class. Better standards prevailed – 90 per cent of all tourist cabins had a private toilet and shower. Used in trans-ocean service between Cuxhaven (Hamburg), Southampton, Cherbourg and New York, she attracted considerable attention for reviving West Germany's largest liner to date. (The 32,200grt *Bremen*, also rebuilt having been the former French *Pasteur* in her first life, surpassed her a year later, in July 1959.) The *Hanseatic*'s actual tonnage increased from 26,313 to 30,029 and – with the addition of a new bow – her length from 666ft to 672ft.

During the winter months and increasingly throughout the year, especially after the first jet flights began in October 1958 and Atlantic liner services began their long, but steady decline, the *Hanseatic* turned to cruising. Her itineraries were diverse: from New York to Bermuda, Nassau and the Caribbean; from Port Everglades (Fort Lauderdale) to the Caribbean; from Cuxhaven on summer trips to the North Cape and Baltic, and in winter to Madeira and the Canaries; and on steadily popular flysail cruises from Genoa around the Mediterranean and out to West Africa.

Her end was untimely, however. While loading passengers at New York's Pier 84, on 7 September 1966, she caught fire. Smoke poured out over the river from windows, portholes and ventilators. Firefighters poured water onto the burning ship, but were especially cautious. They did not want to repeat the *Normandie* fire and have the ship overloaded with water and capsize. With her sailing to Europe cancelled and her passengers sent over instead to the likes of the nearby *Queen Mary*, the scorched *Hanseatic* was later towed over to the Todd shipyard in Brooklyn's Eire Basin for inspection and possible preliminary repairs. But the stench of smoke had permeated throughout much of the 36-year-old ship and so any thought of repairs were abandoned. Within weeks, on 10 October, she was towed to Hamburg and delivered to local scrappers. Some fittings were removed first, such as deck chairs which were sent over to the *Homeric* of the affiliate Home Lines. Hamburg Atlantic itself was revived but as the German Atlantic Line, using the former Israeli *Shalom*, which, in 1968, became the 'new' *Hanseatic*.

Caught in mid river: After the war, the *Empress of Scotland* (ex-*Empress of Japan*) had Canadian Pacific's checker design painted on her three funnels. In this view, during a New York tugboat strike and dated 26 March 1954, the 666ft-long liner is in the Hudson River, about to dock but without the aid of tugs. (Cronican-Arroyo Collection)

Above: Almost unrecognisable, the *Empress of Scotland* was rebuilt as the West German *Hanseatic* in 1958. She became a much more modern-looking liner. (Gillespie-Faber Collection)

Left: Fiery end: The *Hanseatic* afire at New York's Pier 84 in September 1966. (US Coast Guard)

3

COLONIAL SERVICE:
JOHAN VAN OLDENBARNEVELT (1930)

Colonial passenger services were, in ways, unique – they had guaranteed passenger loads with government travellers (from high commissioners and officials and accompanying families, to teachers, missionaries and troops); they also carried the vital mail and cargos; and, altogether, often received generous, government-sponsored operating subsidies. The British passenger fleet had the greatest number of these ships, but others, even if fewer in number, included the likes of the French, Portuguese, Belgians and Dutch. The busiest of the Dutch routes was on the long-haul route out to the East Indies. The Nederland Line and Rotterdam Lloyd dominated this service and both companies were planning new tonnage, their biggest and best ships yet, by the late twenties. Among them was a ship with one of the longest names ever to go to sea: Nederland's *Johan van Oldenbarnevelt*.

One of Holland's most popular and beloved liners, the 19,040grt *Johan van Oldenbarnevelt* was named for the founder of the Dutch East India Company and the 'architect' of Dutch independence following Spanish rule. Her twin sister, with an equally long name, *Marnix van St Aldegonde*, took her name from the chief advisor to William of Orange and the supposed composer of the Dutch national anthem. The pair of 608ft-long liners were the biggest and finest yet for the Amsterdam–Suez–Batavia run and were intended rivals to the new *Boleran* and *Dempo* of rival Rotterdam Lloyd.

Built by Netherlands Shipbuilding Co. in Amsterdam, the *Johan van Oldenbarnevelt* – often referred to more simply and affectionately as the '*JVO*' – was launched on 3 August 1929 and ready for her sea trials in the spring of 1930. Designed with a 17-knot service speed provided by twin, Swiss-made Sulzer diesels, she did a very pleasing 19 knots on trials. Once handed over to her owners, she had a special duty: a short cruise with very distinguished guests from Amsterdam to IJmuiden and return. The occasion was the dedication and opening of the new North Sea Lock, then the largest sea lock in the world, in the North Sea Canal. The guest list was headed by Her Majesty Queen Wilhelmina, Prince Hendrik and their daughter, Crown Princess Juliana. Few liners have started their careers as something of a royal yacht.

Unfortunately, the maiden sailing to the east was far more dramatic. After leaving Amsterdam on 6 May, the *JVO* collided with a Dutch freighter, the *Reggestroom*. Shipyard crews worked night and day, and had the liner repaired

Colonial service: The 19,040grt *Johan van Oldenbarnevelt* docked at Tandjung Priok, the port for Batavia (present-day Jakarta). (Nedlloyd)

Rich, dark decor: The Music Room aboard the *JVO*. (Nedlloyd)

flexible – 245 to 300 in first class, 246 to 367 in second class, 64 to 99 in third class, but a fixed 48 in fourth class. The accommodation ranged from two deluxe suites – with bedroom, sitting room and full bathroom – up in first class to austere dormitories adjoining the crew quarters for fourth class. Every cabin was either outside or located along well-ventilated corridors, however. In addition, the *JVO* could carry up to 1,000 tons of cargo in five holds and which was serviced by no less than a dozen three-ton deck cranes that sat all along the open decks. Raised in position, these cranes looked like mounted guns. Another onlooker thought of them as raised oars aboard a sailing ship.

The *JVO* was a blend of Dutch and East Indian styles. One brochure announced, 'She reflected the wealth and brilliance of the East Indies'. The Smoking Room, for example, was done in chocolate brown panelling covered in antique gold leather. All of the furniture was done in ebony, with inlays of tin in most of the chairs. The ceiling was done in a red copper tone and rose above beams of beaten copper. The two-deck-high Social Hall was lined in padouk, again inlaid with tin and with carved teak doors and panels completing the decor. The dining room was done in white-painted mahogany and included a tapestry at the far end depicting old Amsterdam.

In the politically tense summer of 1939, the *JVO* had a special duty: she was quickly chartered to the Holland America Line for an evacuation crossing to New York. Detoured to Rotterdam, she was booked to absolute capacity for the westbound leg; she returned to Europe with as few as

in three days and off on her scheduled voyage. Using her reserve speed and cutting, as well as reducing, port calls, she reached Batavia on time.

The *JVO* was normally routed from Amsterdam and Southampton to Gibraltar/Algiers, Palma/Villefranche, Genoa, Port Said, Colombo, Sabang, Belawan Deli, Singapore and Batavia. Fares to Batavia from Southampton were posted as £88 in first class, £64 in second class and £50 in third class.

The *JVO* had six main passenger decks, which included such facilities as a full hospital, swimming pool, gymnasium (located just ahead of the forward funnel), a nursery, music room, three dining rooms and considerable open-air promenade deck space. The latter was especially useful for steamy passages through the Red Sea and across the Indian Ocean. The berthing was

Dutch style: Passengers settle in an outside, double-bedded stateroom. Such quarters offered great comfort for the long voyage out to the East Indies. (Rotterdam Maritime Museum)

twenty-nine passengers. With security at sea uncertain, the *JVO* and her sister were hereafter rerouted via South Africa, stopping at Cape Town and Durban en route to and from Batavia. This was soon to change, however – beginning in early 1940, she was based at Genoa, in still-neutral Italy. Dutch passengers were transported by rail. When Rotterdam was bombed on 14 May 1940 and Holland seized, the homeward-bound *JVO* was ordered to reverse course and return to the Indies, and was quickly registered at Batavia. Everything changed yet further – she and several other Dutch liners were transferred to the Java–New York Line, which ran emergency sailings between New York, other US East Coast ports, the South African Cape and the East Indies. Passengers had become less of a priority whereas cargo was more pressing, even urgent. Important cargos of US-bound rubber were aboard. On the *JVO*, freight was even stacked in the public rooms. Then, still more pressing duties – the ship was converted at still-neutral New York to a 4,000-capacity troopship, re-registered at Curaçao in the Dutch West Indies, allocated to the British Ministry of Transport and managed by the Orient Line, a London-headquartered company long experienced with passenger liners and their operations. In all, the *JVO* had an impressive wartime record: thirty-three voyages, 281,000 miles and transporting over 72,000 passengers.

While the *Marnix van St Aldegonde* was bombed and sunk off Algeria in November 1943, the *JVO* heroically survived and returned to Holland – to Rotterdam in August 1945 and to Amsterdam in March 1946. There was little time to restore her, however, as the ship was called up by the Dutch Government – carrying troops out to troubled Indonesia and then returning with evacuees. In between, there was other work to do – transporting fare-assisted Dutch migrants out to new lives in either Australia or South Africa.

In 1951–52, she was made over as a full-time migrant ship – transformed from the original 770 passengers in four classes to 1,414 in a single, all-tourist class configuration. The cabin accommodation was rearranged completely with very few double or triple rooms, but mostly 200 four-berth cabins, 50 five- to six-berth and no less than 13 large dormitories. All the cabins were fitted with washstands, but with cold running water only. Added amenities included a cinema, hairdressing salons and two self-service passenger laundries. She had her problems as well: engine troubles, delayed sailings, more than a few, if small, fires and growing problems with cockroaches. She was also detoured on occasion in the 1950s, running student, migrant and low-fare tourist sailings on the Atlantic, to New York, Halifax and Quebec City. These voyages were looked after by the Holland America Line and were usually offered in the peak summer travel season. Jeanette Moran, then a young college student bound for a summer of European travels, recalled:

> We sailed from Hoboken on the *JVO* in the summer of 1958. The ship was dark, very hot and – according to an officer – all but over-booked. She was crammed, mostly with students like myself and some teachers and older adults as chaperones. The ship was slow and I seem to remember it taking as much as 10 days to reach Amsterdam. It was all great fun, cheap of course, but not especially comfortable. Down on the lower decks, it was an inferno. It took the ship 2 or 3 days just to cool down.

With passenger loads beginning to decline and with old East Indian trade all but vanished, the Nederland Line (with the *JVO* as well as its flagship, the *Oranje*) and Royal Rotterdam Lloyd (with their *Willem Ruys*) decided on a monthly around-the-world service. Given another extended refit, with her capacity now revised to 1,210 (all one class), bathrooms were fitted to some cabins, dormitory quarters were reduced, a second pool was installed and the prized amenity of air conditioning was added. She had a new, modernised exterior look as well: a grey hull, domed funnels and the twin masts replaced by one above the wheelhouse. The *JVO*'s new routing was eastbound world voyages: Amsterdam, Southampton, Palma de Majorca, Genoa, Port Said,

A little like Amsterdam afloat: The Smoking Room aboard the 770-passenger JVO. The decor was a reminder of the homeland. (Nedlloyd)

Reconditioned in 1959 and given heightened, domed tops to her funnels, the 609ft-long JVO passes through the Panama Canal on the homeward leg of an around-the-world voyage. (Nedlloyd)

Suez, Colombo, Fremantle, Melbourne, Sydney, Wellington, Auckland, Suva, Papeete, Callao, Cristobal, Port Everglades, occasionally New York and then return to Southampton and Amsterdam. The minimum fare in 1959 was $975 for the three-month voyage. Unfortunately, it was all less than a success – within three years, the JVO was for sale. Her last assignment for the Dutch was a charter: being used as a moored hotel at Perth in Australia for the Seventh Commonwealth Games.

In February 1963, after sailing empty to Europe, the JVO was handed over to new owners: the Greek Line. Modernised yet again, at a Genoa shipyard, her public areas were given Greek-themed decorations, one pool and lido area was extended, and the cabins were upgraded. She was renamed Lakonia for year-round cruising: sailing from Southampton on twelve- to sixteen-night voyages, mostly to Spain, Portugal, West Africa and the Atlantic Isles. She was scheduled for seventeen cruises between April and November 1963, and twenty-seven trips between Christmas 1963 and November 1964. In winter, she was teamed with another aged, much refitted liner, the Arkadia, which had been the Monarch of Bermuda of 1931.

Plagued with engine problems and often one to three days off schedule, the Lakonia developed a certain popularity and was fully booked for her Christmas cruise in 1963. Sadly, this was to be her very last voyage. The day before reaching Madeira, on 22 December, fire broke out in the hairdressing salon and spread rapidly. The ship was quickly filled with smoke. The initial problems included a lack of fire detection and then the slow response to the fire itself. An SOS was finally flashed to all nearby ships, including the liner Independence. Evacuating the 33-year-old less than perfectly maintained Lakonia was chaotic and very troublesome: some lifeboats were lowered with great difficulty, others leaked once they reached the chilly waters of the Atlantic, and then a davit collapsed, dropping a fully loaded lifeboat into the sea. By midnight the next day, the Lakonia was burning from end to end.

Survivors were later rescued, picked up from lifeboats, rafts and life rings, from rescue ships, which included two passenger ships, Belgium's Charlesville and the Stratheden of P&O. The smouldering, smoking Lakonia was left to drift and burn herself out. On the next day, Christmas Eve, two tugs attempted to put her under tow and then slowly make for Gibraltar. Soon, the burnt-out liner began to list and then finally heeled over and sank on 29 December. The long and varied career of the Johan van Oldenbarnevelt, one of the most interesting liners of the 1930s, was over.

4

MIGHT, STYLE AND SPLENDOUR: *EMPRESS OF BRITAIN* (1931)

The French added the stunning *Île de France* in 1927, then the Germans – in almost extraordinary revival from the ruins of the First World War – added not one but two super liners, the *Bremen* and *Europa* in 1929–30. On the drawing boards, there were also two big liners for the Italians and, largest of all, super ships for Cunard, White Star and the French Line (the White Star ship would be cancelled, however). The Wall Street Crash in October 1929, the start of the worldwide Depression and the 50 per cent slump in transatlantic passenger traffic seemed to cause few changes. Spirits and therefore future projections for new liners, some of the most lavish yet, were high.

The great Canadian Pacific Company had the prestigious distinction of 'spanning the world' – transatlantic by liner from Britain to Eastern Canada, across North America by rail and then a second fleet of liners on the Pacific that went from Vancouver to the Orient. The beautiful, white-hulled Empress liners were perhaps at the lead in this vast organisation and operation. The Pacific service had just been topped by the aforementioned *Empress of Japan*, a 26,000-tonner commissioned in 1930. She was one of the finest liners on the Pacific and also the fastest.

Canadian Pacific also planned a second liner, even bigger and more lavish than the *Empress of Japan*. She was the 42,000-ton *Empress of Britain*. The 748ft-long ship was built by the renowned John Brown shipyard on the Clyde and was launched on 11 June 1930, after being named by the then very popular Prince of Wales (who later became Edward VIII and then the Duke of Windsor). There was added distinction to the occasion: for the first time in history, launch proceedings were broadcast throughout the British Empire and, rather expectedly, to Canada and the United States.

Carrying comparatively few passengers (1,195 with 465 in first class, 260 in tourist and 470 in third class), the new *Empress* was Britain's biggest liner in almost twenty years, since the *Aquitania* of 1914. Her long, white hull was doubly strengthened for ice (for nine months of the year she would ply the North Atlantic between Southampton, Cherbourg and Quebec City). She had five holds as well – three for general cargo, the fourth for insulated goods and the last for passenger baggage. On the outside, her designers opted for unusually mammoth funnels, which were in deep contrast to her owners' initial desire for more normal-sized ones. Together with a well-balanced, almost orderly, superstructure, the three giant stacks added considerably to overall senses of size, power and security. In daylight, she presented a most handsome form and great ocean liner style, and altogether unquestionably

Empress of Britain: World cruise visit to Melbourne, winter 1939. (ALF Collection)

22   GREAT PASSENGER SHIPS: 1930-1940

A grand liner: The 42,300grt *Empress of Britain* – with her imposing three funnels – passes under the Golden Gate Bridge at San Francisco during the final month of her winter world cruise. (Canadian Pacific)

California and the Panama Canal before making a springtime return to Manhattan. Her capacity for these cruises, which became standards for 1930s luxury travel, was reduced from 1,195 to 700 all first class. She became more club-like. Considering her size, she offered passengers an unparalleled amount of space per passenger.

The *Empress of Britain* made headlines and featured in newsreels when she brought King George VI and Queen Elizabeth (later the Queen Mother) home from their highly successful friendship-building North American tour in 1939. The royal couple had crossed to Canada weeks before, but on another Canadian Pacific liner, the *Empress of Australia*. Dowager Queen Mary and the little princesses, Elizabeth (later HM the

ranked as one of the great liners of the 1930s; at night, with her buff funnels floodlit, her appearance became even more dramatic and imposing.

Her innards were, in a word, sumptuous. There was the columned, traditional Mayfair Lounge, which could be contrasted against the angular, stunningly modern, very art deco Cathay Lounge. The Salle Jacques was ranked as one of the finest shipboard restaurants while the Empress Ballroom and The Mall became established shipboard spaces. There was a large indoor pool, a gymnasium and a full squash court located on the highest deck, between the funnels.

The *Empress* was built from the start with the added intention of spending each winter as a cruise ship and, more specifically, as a world cruise ship. Each January, she would leave New York's Chelsea Piers, with her outer propellers specially removed to reduce drag and save fuel, for as long as 140 days – for the Mediterranean, Suez, India, the Dutch East Indies, Hong Kong, China, Japan and then homeward across the Pacific to Hawaii,

Art deco styling: The entrance to the First Class Dining Room aboard the 1,195-passenger *Empress of Britain*. (Canadian Pacific)

Queen) and Margaret, greeted their parents upon arrival at Southampton. However glamorous and exciting this was, and however much it added to the ship's other distinctions, she was not a great financial success. She failed to build a strong, even an added, following among Canada-routed passengers (most travellers still preferring the New York route). Those long world cruises were victims of both the ongoing Depression and simply the vast, added expense of running such luxurious jaunts.

The *Empress* left Southampton on 2 September 1939, the day after the peace-breaking invasion of Poland. She had far more passengers aboard than normal. Evacuees and frightened, often desperate, tourists without actual cabin accommodation were assigned to cots set up in the public rooms and even in a special arrangement on the squash court. Once at Quebec City, she was temporarily laid up – pending further decision by the Admiralty. Two months later, in November, she was formally called to duty. Repainted in grey, she sailed to Clydebank, the place of her birth, for refitting as a high-capacity troopship. She then made two more sailings to Canada, bringing servicemen over to Britain. In March 1940, she was dispatched to far-off waters, to New Zealand. Briefly, she sailed in convoy with the *Queen Mary*, *Aquitania* and other liner-troopers far removed from their peacetime runs. The *Empress*'s spell in southern climates was quite short, however.

The *Empress* was returning home to England, via Cape Town and Freetown, on 26 October when she was attacked and set afire by Nazi bombers. One of the bombs made a direct hit on the once splendid Mayfair Lounge. Sadly, she was only 70 miles north-west of Ireland at the time. She burned from end to end. All but forty-nine of her 600 passengers and crew were saved, however. The blistering hulk was finally put under tow by the Polish destroyer *Burza*. But two days later, on 28 October, the Nazi submarine *U-32* sighted the former liner and fired two torpedoes. The once great *Empress* sank quickly. Some reports suggested that Hitler himself had ordered the ship to be sunk because of her association with the King, Queen and their alliance-building trip a year and a half before. In the final accounting, she became the largest Allied merchant ship to be lost in the Second World War.

Three blasts: Time for another gala departure by the *Empress of Britain*. (Canadian Pacific)

Taking a break between sailings, the mighty, 758ft-long *Empress of Britain* rests in the King George V Graving Dock, the largest dock of its kind in the world in the 1930s. (Canadian Pacific)

5

LONG-LASTING LINER: *MONTEREY* (1932)

In October 1931, when the *Monterey* was launched at Quincy, Massachusetts, the managers and directors (of the San Francisco-based Matson Line) and the designers and building crews (of Bethlehem Steel) could never have imagined that the 632ft-long passenger liner would be around for sixty-nine years. What good fortune! What history! And what a tribute to shipbuilding and design! In her last life, the *Monterey* sailed as the *Britanis* of the Chandris Line and, even at age 60, was making twice-weekly cruises out of Miami and also an annual seven-week trip around continental South America. Her amazing record was also a tribute to Chandris, who sailed her and who so impeccably and lovingly maintained her.

'She is in very good condition – very strong and very solid', according to one of her final Greek masters, Captain George Panagiotakis. The captain was interviewed in 1992, at the time of the ship's 60th birthday, and continued:

We are still using the original steam turbines. Of course, they require almost constant maintenance. We repair and replace parts immediately. And even though most of the original manufacturers are out of business, we do not have much of a problem with spares. We even have them custom-made if necessary, usually in the United States, but also in the UK and in Greece. Some other parts have come from her near-sister *Ellinis*, scrapped in 1987, but which had been the original Matson *Lurline*, built in 1932 and a sister ship to the *Monterey*. In fact, the *Ellinis* had parts from the *Homeric*, which was the third Matson sister, the *Mariposa* of 1931. So you might say that all three Matson sisters live-on in the *Britanis*.

The Captain added proudly:

We still average 19½ knots, and sometimes 21. Onboard, we need good steam engineers. There are, in fact, three steam-driven liners left in the Chandris fleet [1992] – *Britanis*, *Amerikanis* and *Meridian*. We dry dock the *Britanis* at Norfolk for three weeks every two years.

We have 12 boilers onboard – six for each funnel. Each week, we take on bunkers – 200–250 tons of heavy fuel and 40 tons of diesel oil. We also take on 2,500 tons of water.

Captain Panagiotakis had first joined the *Britanis* in 1971, on the original Chandris liner service between Europe and Australia:

It took four weeks to sail from Southampton to Sydney via South Africa. We were usually routed via Lisbon, Las Palmas or Tenerife, Cape Town, then across to Fremantle, Melbourne and Sydney. From Sydney, we would sometimes make a cruise with Australians and to places like Suva, Lautoka, Apia and Papeete. These would be two-week voyages. Afterward, we would resume the 'line voyage' via Wellington, Tahiti, Acapulco, the Panama Canal, San Juan, Port Everglades and finally home to Southampton. The full voyage would take 6075 days. Outbound, we'd sail completely full – 1,600 migrants bound for Australia. Homewards, we would be about 75 per cent full – almost 1,200 passengers – and this was mostly budgeted tourists and backpackers and large families on holiday.

The *Britanis* was first commissioned in April 1932, having been built especially for Matson Line's South Seas liner route: San Francisco and Los Angeles to Hawaii, the South Pacific islands, New Zealand and Australia. As the *Monterey*, she was paired with the *Mariposa*. They were said to be two of the very finest liners in Pacific service. The *Lurline* (and a somewhat smaller companion, the *Malolo*) looked after the Hawaiian run.

LONG-LASTING LINER: *MONTEREY* (1932)   25

Below: The Main Lounge aboard the *Lurline,* the third of the big Matson liners of the 1930s. (Matson Line)

Above: The Monteray in 1932 undergoing a last check at the Boston Naval Yard. (ALF Collection)

26 GREAT PASSENGER SHIPS: 1930-1940

Matson style: The First Class Dining Room aboard the *Monterey*'s twin sistership, the *Mariposa*. (Matson Line)

Outbound on a 'cruise to nowhere,' the *Britanis* (ex-*Monterey*, ex-*Matsonia*, ex-*Lurline*) passes the Lower Manhattan skyline. The date is 1985. (Chandris Cruises)

America's entry into the Second World War, in December 1941, disrupted these services and, with a heroic record of long passengers, hundreds of thousands of troops and even a major rescue, the *Monterey* was returned to Matson, but then sent directly to 'mothballs'. It seemed that restoration costs were unaffordable, at least until the mid-1950s when she was modernised and upgraded as the 'new' *Matsonia*. She had her debut in May 1957, and – carrying 760 all first-class passengers – was placed on the Honolulu route with the highly popular *Lurline*. In 1963, however, when her running-mate was withdrawn, she took on the more popular name and, in fact, became Matson's last liner to be called *Lurline*. Chandris bought her in 1970.

The *Britanis* began cruising full-time in 1975 (first divided between European and Caribbean itineraries) and was in permanent US service from 1981. Captain Panagiotakis recalled:

> At first, we did mostly short cruises and mostly out of New York. We sailed up to Halifax, Martha's Vineyard, Boston, New London and even attended the America's Cup Races at Newport. We also had luncheon cruises from New York, from 9.30 in the morning until 2.30 in the afternoon. Now [1992], we are the only ship making two-night cruises out of Miami over to Nassau and back. These are 'party cruises' – very popular for dancing, drinking and gambling.

When we last cruised on the *Britanis* in the summer of 1992, she was still glowing. She was 'snow white' from stem to stern, and was rather unique in being capped by a pair of distinctive blue and white stacks. Estimates by Chandris engineers that she might sail for another ten years proved overly optimistic. Retired in 1995, she did a stint – under charter to the US Government – as a refugee detention centre in Cuba. Laid up afterward as the renamed *Belophin*, there was some talk of making her into an art deco-themed hotel moored along the San Francisco waterfront in 1998. But that expensive project never came to pass. In 2000, without hope, she was finally sold to Indian scrap merchants. Her end came sooner, however. While being towed around South Africa, in October, the otherwise empty liner took on water, began to sink by the stern and finally, with her bow pointed upwards, took her final plunge.

6

SAILING COASTAL: AMERICAN 'MINI LINERS'

In the early 1980s, many elderly, unused and often neglected steamer piers along the New York City waterfront were demolished. Two of them, Piers 34 and 36, at the foot of Spring Street in Lower Manhattan, were among those pulled down. Their disappearance was barely noticed, however. They were, in fact, a link to a long-ago part of American merchant shipping: the coastal passenger liners. Those piers belonged to the long vanished Clyde Mallory Lines, which had one of the most extensive fleets of 'mini liners'.

It might be difficult to imagine that in this age of fast airline flights that travellers once sailed on these 'mini liners' between New York and US East Coast ports such as Charleston, Jacksonville and Miami. They also took steamers northwards to Nova Scotia in summer and had overnight excursions to Boston. It was a glorious age in American shipping that reached its peak in the 1930s. Even if the harsh Depression still raged, these short trips on little luxury liners provided ideal escapism. Sadly, however, it all just about disappeared after the Second World War, a victim of increased airline competition, greater auto travel and, with trucks using new and expanding highways, losing cargo as well.

The late Rupert Ferguson remembered 'sailing coastal':

I joined the Eastern Steamship Lines back in 1926, as a cashier on the Boston to Bangor, Maine overnight run. We had passengers, of course, but also sometimes horses as well. Later, I went on the Boston-St John, New Brunswick run and then to the New York–Boston overnight service. I also sailed on the Old Dominion Line on their New York–Norfolk passenger run and on which we often carried lots of mail. Sometimes, the mail was delivered to the ship at the last minute – it arrived by taxi even if it was only one sack! In 1935–36, passenger fares for these overnight voyages ranged from 75 cents for a minimum cabin down on the lowest deck and with upper and lower bunks to $8 for the very best stateroom with twin beds and private bathroom on the Saloon Deck.

Rupert Ferguson later went on the busy Miami–Havana overnight run:

I was aboard Eastern Steamship's *Evangeline*, one of the crack coastal ships of her day. We'd have three trips a week with a one-night layover. We ran opposite the *Florida*, a steamer owned by the local P&O Steamship Lines and no relation to the big British shipping firm. P&O in Florida was part of the Flagler system, which included hotels and railways. Otherwise, there was only the Pan Am Clippers, the famed 'flying boats,' in those days.

Clyde Mallory Lines was not only one of the biggest but one of the finest firms in the coastal trades in the 1920s and '30s. They also owned some of the best fitted ships, such as the 6,200grt, 18-knot sister ships *Shawnee* and *Iroquois*. Certainly 'baby ocean liners' with twin masts and a pair of raked 'paint can' stacks, they boasted luxurious salons, top-class restaurants and comfortable cabins. They carried 600 passengers each and, of course, cargo – general cargo, automobiles and fresh fruit coming north from Florida. Rupert Ferguson joined the 409ft-long *Shawnee* as assistant purser in 1937:

We were on the New York-Jacksonville-Miami run. We'd leave New York at noon on Saturdays and then arrive in Jacksonville on Mondays and at Miami on Tuesdays. We'd be back in New York again on Friday afternoons. I especially remember that on Thursdays, on the northbound *Shawnee*, the larger Ward Line cruise ship *Oriente* would always overtake us. She was coming from Havana and, of course, was a sister to the ill-fated *Morro Castle*, which we used to see as a burnt-out hulk and lying on the beach at Asbury Park, New Jersey, in 1934. At New York, we used Pier 34, close to Canal Street.

We'd have lots of one-way passengers on these sailings to Florida aboard *Shawnee*. Some left at Jacksonville to go to the Florida West Coast resorts, others on tours to Sea Island in Georgia and still others to local hotels. At Miami, they

During her career in the 1930s with the Clyde Mallory Lines, the 6,200grt *Iroquois* had a black hull for a time before being repainted in a more cruise-like light grey. (Everett Viez Collection)

Rushing home: The *Iroquois* was used to evacuate passengers, especially Americans, out of Europe and after war had been declared in the fall of 1939. With 776 anxious passengers aboard, she is seen on 11 October 1939 as the 409ft-long little liner nears the safety of New York harbour. (Cronican-Arroyo Collection)

could have a 14-day trip – a week ashore in Florida and a combined 7 days on the ship. Often, I remember the same passengers coming back aboard the northbound trips. They'd gotten too much sun – some looked like lobsters! At Miami, in those pre-Dodge Island, big cruise ship days, we'd dock at the foot of 10th Street and Biscayne Boulevard. The *Shawnee* and her sister were, of course, different style ships than today's amenity-filled cruise ships. There were no showers in the cabins, for example, and certainly no air-conditioning. Outside cabins with open portholes were preferred. Passengers in often steamy inside cabins were allowed to sleep on deck weather-permitting, of course. I do also recall all sorts of curious passengers. One rich woman stored her false teeth in the iced water of her Champagne bucket and another stayed in the pool during lifeboat drills. On the sadder side, I remember a broken businessman who committed suicide off the Florida coast because it was the place he liked best and another, with financial problems, who took out a revolver and suddenly started firing at passengers on the open decks.

Life for the *Shawnee* and all other coastal liners began to change with the sudden outbreak of war in Europe in the autumn of 1939. Rupert Ferguson concluded:

While at New York and preparing for another routine trip to Florida, we were suddenly chartered to the United States Lines for transatlantic evacuation service. But because we were such a small ship and one never intended to make a big ocean crossing, we needed extra ballast. So, the ship was fitted with cobblestones – Belgian cobblestones and the kind used in New York

SAILING COASTAL: AMERICAN 'MINI-LINERS'

City streets. We went empty to the Atlantic coast of France and then waited at anchor before taking on a full load of anxious, worried passengers. They were desperate to get out of Europe. There were such demands on this little liner that water rationing was down to three hours each day. We sailed to New York with specially painted neutrality markings along our sides and, at night, we were always well lighted to show our colors and ward off lurking Nazi subs.

When the war ended, in 1945, the coastal services on these little liners were all but finished. The likes of the Old Dominion and Clyde Mallory lines were disbanded, ships such as the *Shawnee* were sold off – the *Shawnee* to become the foreign flag *City of Lisbon* and later the *Partizanka* and the *Evangeline* put into post-war cruise service. A glorious if different part of ocean travel had ended.

Above: Busy times: New York's Chelsea Piers are all but crammed with passenger ships. The *Shawnee*, *Acadia* and *St John* are at the top, each of them hurriedly called to duty to evacuate passengers from troubled Europe. Just below are the *Uruguay*, *Washington*, *President Harding*, *American Traveler* and *American Merchant*. The date is 23 September 1939. (Port Authority of New York & New Jersey)

Below: Intended for service to New England and the Canadian Maritimes from Boston as well as New York, the 5,000grt *Yarmouth* is seen in a view dated 30 May 1934. (Everett Viez Collection)

30 GREAT PASSENGER SHIPS: 1930–1940

The little 400-passenger Turkish liner *Ankara*, the former *Iroquois*, was the last of the noted American coastal passenger ships when she was scrapped at Aliaga, Turkey. The date is 20 July 1982 and just behind is another Turkish passenger ship, the 6,700grt *Iskenderun*. (Selim San)

7

ITALIAN SUPER LINER: *CONTE DI SAVOIA* (1932)

Soon after the Second World War ended, and in the first months of 1946, there was some potentially bright news out of war-ravaged, impoverished Italy. Inspection teams from Italian Line's Genoa headquarters were looking over the burnt-out wreckage of the once glorious 1930s super liner *Conte di Savoia*. With her 814ft-long hull found to be in solid condition and with encouraging reports on the state of her once powerful steam turbine machinery (that had produced a service speed of a racy 27 knots), it all seemed hopeful. With almost all of Italian Line's great pre-war fleet in ruins (including the larger *Rex*) and with four surviving liners then still in American hands (and with no guarantee of their return by 1946), the company was all but desperate to restore at least some of its pre-war passenger services.

Maurizio Eliseo, the author of numerous books on Italian liners and himself one of the greatest archivists of Italian passenger ship history, reported:

> Drawings of the rebuilt *Conte di Savoia* were made at the Genoa headquarters. She would have been changed – with one funnel in a center position. The original three-class quarters would have been changed to 3,000 to 3,500 and all in third class, all immigrants bound from Italy for South America. The plan was to sail her between Naples, Genoa, Lisbon, Rio de Janeiro, Santos, Montevideo and Buenos Aires. Two of the four props would have been removed and she would have been made over as a twin-screw, but slower ship. And those famous gyro-stabilizers would have been removed and converted to storage spaces. But nothing happened in the end. There was no money for such a rebuilding project in Italy at that time and then there were problems with her overall size and capacity, and with her deep draft. Those drawings of a rebuilt *Conte di Savoia* went into the Italian Line basement files and were forgotten.

Originally ordered as the *Dux* and then as the *Conte Azzuro* for Lloyd Sabaudo, another Italian passenger line trading on the mid-Atlantic route to New York. Mussolini had it and two other companies reorganised as the more efficient Italian Line at the height of the Depression, in 1932. Consequently, the 48,500grt ship was finished in staged deference by the Fascists to the Italian royal house as the *Conte di Savoia*. She entered service in the fall of 1932. Running mate to the larger (51,000 tons) and faster *Rex*, that ship seemed to steal more of the publicity especially since it held the prized Blue Riband for two years, from 1933 until 1935.

Together, the *Conte di Savoia* and the *Rex* spent triumphant years on the Italy–New York run, 'the sunny southern route' as it was called. Known for her external good looks, her broad, open-air lido decks and the likes of her extraordinary Colonna Lounge ('like the Sistine Chapel gone to sea' said one

Italy's biggest and grandest liners of the 1930s: the 48,502grt *Conte Di Savoia* is in the center, the 51,062grt *Rex* on the right. They are seen berthed at Genoa and in the typical stern-first docking pattern. (Richard Faber Collection)

32 GREAT PASSENGER SHIPS: 1930–1940

Seen from the deck of the outbound liner *Roma*, the *Conte di Savoia* (left), *Augustus* and *Giulio Cesare* are seen in the background in this view at Genoa. (Paolo Piccione Collection)

The spectacular Colonna Hall aboard the 2,200-passenger *Conte di Savoia*. (Italian Line)

ITALIAN SUPER LINER: *CONTE DI SAVOIA* (1932)

Noted passenger: Cardinal Eugenio Pacelli stands outside the chapel aboard the *Conte di Savoia* during a crossing in October 1936. Cardinal Pacelli became Pope Pius XII in 1939. (Maurizio Eliseo Collection)

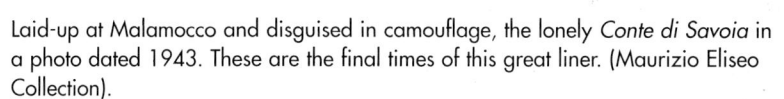

Laid-up at Malamocco and disguised in camouflage, the lonely *Conte di Savoia* in a photo dated 1943. These are the final times of this great liner. (Maurizio Eliseo Collection).

travel writer of the day), the *Conte di Savoia* – which carried 2,200 passengers in four classes – was indeed one of the greatest liners of the pre-war age. But when Italy joined the war, in June 1940, she was laid up at an anchorage at Malamocco, near Venice. Fifty crew looked after the otherwise silent super ship. Sadly, she would never sail again.

Eliseo, who planned a book about the ship, added.

> The *Conte di Savoia* was destroyed when the war in Italy was over and by the Germans – and by mistake. On 8th September 1943, Italy joined the Allied side. By the next morning, the Nazis turned on their former friends and soon they began shooting one another in mass confusion. That day, there was news on Italian radio that 'Savoia' was trying to escape to the south of Italy. The Nazi high command misunderstood and thought of the ship. They sent five bombers to attack her. But actually the radio report referred to a member of the Savoia family, the royal house of Italy. Actually, just before the radio news, the Germans had given orders to move the ship to the Piazza San Marco in Venice for closer control. Actually, she would have been far too deep to dock there.

Eliseo recounted sadly:

After the bombing started, the Germans realized their mistake and orders were given to stop. One bomb hit the Colonna Lounge. The Germans then tried to sink her, but it was too shallow at Malamocco. So she burned down to the main deck. Three days later, on the 12th, Italian Line sent a representative to make the first inspection. While burnt out, he found the hull was still in sound condition.

The blistered hull of the *Conte di Savoia* was refloated later, in 1946, but then remained at Malamocco for another two years. There were reports that the Holland America Line might buy her and then rebuild her for their North Atlantic service as a fleet mate to their *Nieuw Amsterdam*. Nothing came to pass. The French Line was also rumoured to be interested, thinking of rebuilding as well and pairing the ship with the *Île de France* and *Liberté*. Again, nothing materialised. Finally, the *Conte di Savoia* was towed to Monfalcone, to the shipyard that is today Fincantieri and where large, modern cruise ships are built, for scrapping. She was docked in the fitting-out berth.

The remains of the *Conte di Savoia* were still being dismantled in 1950, just as the brand-new, 27,000-ton *Giulio Cesare* was building just across the way. Together, the two liners represented two generations of great Italian passenger ships.

8

THE HONEYMOON SHIP: *QUEEN OF BERMUDA* (1933)

'She was one of the most popular and familiar liners ever to sail from New York,' recalled Ian Robertson, a one-time cabin steward aboard the *Queen of Bermuda*. He continued:

> She was in port, at Pier 95, arriving almost every Friday, staying overnight and then, like clockwork, sailing precisely at 3 on Saturday afternoons. She had booming steam whistles that signaled her departure, tugs positioning her out into Hudson River. She always looked impeccable – elegantly making her way down the Hudson and often in company with her running-mate, the smaller but yacht-like *Ocean Monarch*. They made a great team – and were proud members of the then mighty British ocean liner fleet.

When the Furness-Bermuda Line ordered their 19,000-ton *Bermuda*, it was not only the firm's biggest ship but also something of a gamble. It was estimated that the weekly New York–Bermuda passenger run would be seasonal at best and that the 691-passenger *Bermuda* might have to spend considerable time finding employment elsewhere (most likely on longer cruises to the Caribbean). However, soon after this first-class liner entered service in 1927, the result was an overwhelming success. The tiny island, located just some 600 miles south of New York, was coming into its own as a tourist spot – and so the demand for passages exceeded even the wildest expectations at Furness. Within a short space of time, the company turned its attention to an even bigger liner, the 22,000-ton *Mid-Ocean*, which could easily supplement the earlier vessel.

Such well-intended plans went completely astray in June 1931, however, when the 4-year-old *Bermuda* burned at her Hamilton berth. Then, as if to deliberately complicate matters, she was scorched a second time at the Belfast repair yard. Afterward, she was worthy only for the scrappers. Rather quickly, a new set of plans were put in order. The *Mid-Ocean* was given a fresh image and in the process, while still building, was given a new name: *Monarch of Bermuda*. At least three other liners were temporarily chartered to fill the voids in Furness-Bermuda scheduling, including Cunard's *Franconia*, Holland–America's *Veendam* and the Canadian Pacific *Duchess of Bedford*. Then, in great enthusiasm and projection, a second, brand-new liner was ordered from the Vickers-Armstrong yard at Barrow-in-Furness, which was to become the *Queen of Bermuda*.

The *Monarch of Bermuda* first appeared at the end of 1931, and was followed by the 580ft-long *Queen of Bermuda* two years later, in February 1933.

Following her post-war refit in 1947–48, the stately *Queen of Bermuda* passes the famed Liverpool skyline. The Royal Liver, Cunard and Docks & Harbour Board buildings – the noted 'Three Graces' – rise in the background. (Richard Faber Collection)

THE HONEYMOON SHIP: QUEEN OF BERMUDA (1933) 35

A day at Hamilton, Bermuda with the near sisters *Queen of Bermuda* (left) and *Monarch of Bermuda* alongside at the same time. (Author's Collection)

As something of a well-publicised 'royal pair,' they settled down quickly to a luxury cruise trade not paralleled at the time in short-haul sea travel. The two liners could carry as many as 1,500 passengers to the island each, mostly on six-night cruises and with a forty-hour passage in each direction and three full days docked in downtown Hamilton. With the combination of their crisp service, rich appointments and precision timetables, they were soon dubbed 'the Millionaires' ships'. Furthermore, they were quite unique in their day – there was private plumbing in every stateroom. And as for their frequent Saturday afternoon departures, a strong following developed from the 'just married' set. There was another dubbing: they were the 'honeymoon ships'.

The Second World War sent the *Queen* hurrying back to Britain, painted in drab grey and soon quickly outfitted for military duties. She was given nine guns, protective outer plating and had her holds filled with empty barrels for added flotation if attacked. The third funnel came off in the process, a dummy and most likely a form of added disguise (only to be returned after the war ended).

The post-war Furness-Bermuda plan was to reactivate the popular pair, but then the *Monarch of Bermuda* was heavily damaged by fire while undergoing her restoration refit. She was ultimately sold off to the British Government, turned into an austere immigrant carrier for the UK–Australia run as the *New Australia* and finally passed, in 1957, to the Greek

Shipboard splendor: The beautiful, two-deck-high Forum Lounge aboard the 22,500grt *Queen of Bermuda*. (Author's Collection)

36 GREAT PASSENGER SHIPS: 1930–1940

Line and became their *Arkadia*. The *Queen* was far more fortunate, however – even if something of a Victoria without her Albert. Fully restored to her luxurious self, she left Manhattan's Pier 95 on her first post-war sailing to Bermuda. Coincidentally, the sailing was on Valentine's Day. Her success story resumed immediately.

The *Queen of Bermuda* was given a consort in 1951, in the form of the smaller, more yacht-like 13,500-ton *Ocean Monarch*. As a new team, a sort of regularity was quickly established with Saturday afternoon sailings promptly at 3 o'clock. Honeymooners – along with film stars, businessmen and their families, general tourists and, in summer, schoolteachers – could rejoice. The most popular offering was the six-day 'live aboard' cruise where the ship served as the hotel in Bermuda. Minimum round-trip fares in the 1950s began at $150. Alternatively, other passengers elected to sail southbound, spend a week or two in a Bermuda hotel and then return by sea – or even aboard the other Furness liner.

Furness decided on a facelift for their beloved *Queen* in 1961 and sent her to Belfast for a long winter overhaul. She returned almost unrecognisable: The original three funnels were gone and replaced with one large, tapered type (and this giving the unusual liner distinction of having sailed as a one-, two- and three-funnel ship). Full air conditioning was installed throughout her wood-panelled innards as well.

Time was running short, however. Several cruise ship disasters in 1965–66, namely disastrous, headline-making fires aboard the *Yarmouth Castle* and *Viking Princess*, prompted the US Coast Guard to bring into effect a new series of stringent safety and especially fire regulations. The ageing *Queen* would need at least another major rebuilding. Instead, her owners – with great reluctance – decided to abandon their traditional Bermuda service altogether. At best, Furness liners, with their 'old world' atmospheres and wooded decor, began to look quaint alongside the likes of the splashy, brand-new *Oceanic*.

While the *Ocean Monarch* was sold off to Bulgarian interests and became the *Varna*, the 33-year-old *Queen of Bermuda* gracefully slipped off, after her final Bermuda sailing in November 1966, to the shipbreakers at Faslane in Scotland.

Far left: Relaxation at sea: The indoor pool aboard the 580ft-long *Queen of Bermuda*. (Author's Collection)

Left: New look: Rebuilt and modernised in 1961–62, the *Queen of Bermuda* had a new, single funnel. (Moran Towing & Transportation Co)

9

THIRTIES DREAMBOATS: *NORMANDIE* (1935) AND *QUEEN MARY* (1936)

The late John Havers was born in Southampton in 1920. His ship-watching hobby developed as a youngster, sparked further by a friend whose father worked for Canadian Pacific:

> My first visits were to the *Empress of Australia*, that grand three-stacker, where we were given a Nestlé's tin of thick milk and a cup of tea [there was no refrigeration onboard many ships at the time]. My enthusiasm soon spread, heightened by a sense of adventure, which included climbing to the crow's nest from inside the foremast.

Young John's world of ships, especially the big liners, soon began to expand rapidly:

> Another family friend worked for the old Southern Railway, which controlled the docks, and who gave us passes for the tenders out to Cowes Roads [an anchorage] to meet the likes of the *Normandie* and the *Bremen*. They also gave us dock passes to board such other liners as the *Aquitania* and *Berengaria*. I think I spent the whole of the 1930s visiting liners. There was so much to see and we wanted to visit every ship. I was especially fond of White Star and their ships, and can recall visiting the *Olympic* just as they were testing her sirens. They were similar to those on her sister, the *Titanic*. Alone, those four stacks were an impressive sight. Each was 81 ½ feet high.

John retained vivid recollections of the great liners of that time:

> I remember the mounted moose heads aboard the *Washington*. There was lots of wicker work aboard the old *Rotterdam*. The *Hansa* had a 'blistered' hull for better balancing at sea. The *Bremen* and *Europa* had very dark woods, which appeared somewhat dull after seeing the likes of spectacular *Normandie*.

However, both of those Germans had exceptional profiles, forerunners to the superb *Nieuw Amsterdam* of 1938.

> The *Normandie* was, of course, the most exceptional ship. She needed a flotilla of tenders. We would meet more film stars on her tenders than those for any other ship. Onboard, she had the distinctive smell of French cigarettes and expensive Parisian perfume. Stepping aboard was a shattering experience. The whole ship seemed to be lacquered gold – gold everywhere – and with a great statue on the staircase descending into the restaurant. Alone, that restaurant could have held one of the Channel steamers of the day. The floors seemed to be a black marble and fountains of light accentuated the richly colored furniture. We even visited the inside of the gigantic third funnel, which was the dog kennel.

> The French Line was very early to experiment with containers for baggage. Great boxes were lifted off the railway cars at Southampton, placed aboard the tenders and then hoisted aboard the *Normandie* by one of her cranes and then dropped down into the forward hold. In almost every way, there was never a ship like the *Normandie*!

The *Normandie* had one noted blemish – vibrations plagued the French flagship in her early years. 'Down in third class,' reported one passenger, 'it was all but unliveable. You were practically "shaken" all the way across the Atlantic.' Newly designed propellers eventually alleviated this problem to some extent. The other problem was, in many ways, far more serious – Britain's brilliant, highly popular *Queen Mary*.

Being built at almost the same time, the 79,280-ton *Normandie* actually came first, in May 1935. Immediately, she captured the Blue Riband with a run of 29.98 knots. The *Rex*'s two-year record of 28.92 knots was surpassed. Along with her extraordinary luxury, her advanced exterior, even her enormous cost (a whopping $60 million), the 1,029ft-long French ship

38 GREAT PASSENGER SHIPS: 1930–1940

Ocean liner royalty: The magnificent *Normandie* departing from New York's Pier 88. (Author's Collection)

Grand gathering: A special day in March 1937 when five noted Atlantic liners were berthed together alongside New York's 'Luxury Liner Row' – the *Europa* (top left) and then the *Rex*, *Normandie*, *Georgic* and *Berengaria*. (Author's Collection)

Longer than the Hall of Mirrors at Versailles, the First Class Dining Room aboard the 82,799grt *Normandie* was nothing short of spectacular. It was a creation of bronze and hammered glass. (Author's Collection)

instantly became headline news. But behind the proud smiles of the French, for Government ministers as well as French Line management, was the nagging threat of the giant new Cunarder. When it was revealed that the *Queen Mary* would be at least 80,000 tons, things turned even more serious. It was evident that the *Normandie* would be displaced to the position of 'world's second largest'. This was unacceptable to the French. Consequently, in her first winter overhaul, in 1935–36, and just months before the *Queen Mary*'s maiden voyage (in May), the French had a large, but otherwise useless, deckhouse constructed on one of the *Normandie*'s aft decks. Almost in a flash, her tonnage jumped to 82,799. She easily surpassed the 80,774 tons listed for the *Queen Mary*. The *Normandie* would remain the largest ship in the world – well, at least for a few more years. When, in February 1940, Cunard's second super ship, the *Queen Elizabeth*, put to sea for the first time, it was bigger still – at 83,673 tons.

There was another big problem that deeply troubled the French – the coveted Blue Riband. Nearly three months following her maiden crossing, in August 1936, the *Queen Mary* snatched the Riband with a run of 30.14 knots. A maritime battle began. The *Normandie* regained the honours in the following March, with a run of 30.9 knots. That summer, she even outdid herself with a recorded 31.2 knots. This fierce rivalry ended altogether, in August 1938, when the *Queen Mary* proved to be the absolute fastest of the two. She crossed at 31.6 knots and afterward held the Riband for fourteen years, until, in July 1952, it went to the *United States*.

The late Everett Viez added:

> The *Normandie* was the most extravagant, luxurious and celebrated liner of her time. Everything about her was extraordinary. Her first-class dining room, filled with bronze, hammered glass and Lalique, was longer than the Hall of Mirrors at Versailles. She had the first complete theatre ever fitted in a liner and the Winter Garden included caged birds and live greenery. Comparatively, the *Queen Mary* was less glamorous, possibly less stunning and certainly less pretentious. She was a classic British liner, comfortable and even cozy in places, decorated in polished woods, sconce lamps, soft chairs and lots of linoleum floors. The Hollywood-like *Normandie* actually inhibited many potential Atlantic travelers, however, and so, in her four-and-half years of service, averaged only 59% of capacity. The *Queen Mary*, on the other hand, was an almost instant favorite and – for her three years until September 1939 – averaged 98% of capacity. While the *Normandie* was Champagne and caviar at midnight, the *Queen Mary* was tea and cakes at four in the afternoon.

Lavish quarters: The bedroom of the Rouen Suite, one of the *Normandie*'s exquisite apartments de luxe. (French Line)

Swimming at midnight: The 80ft-long tiled indoor pool aboard the *Normandie*. (French Line)

The view from the New York Central rail yards of Weehawken, New Jersey. The date is September 1939. The war in Europe has started and liner services are suddenly caught in limbo. The *Roma* (left) is still sailing for Mussolini's Italy, the *Queen Mary* is being repainted in military grey, the *Normandie* is idle (at Pier 88) along with the *Île de France* with the *Champlain* 'nested' alongside. (Author's Collection)

Goddess in ruins: The capsized *Normandie* at Pier 88, days after the devastating fire. (Author's Collection)

The beautiful *Normandie* burning to death on the cold afternoon of 9 February 1942. (Cronican-Arroyo Collection)

Fate for these two great liners differed as well. While the French thought of a running-mate – a super-*Normandie*, a proposed 90,000-tonner that might have been named *Bretagne* – those plans never materialised. The *Normandie* herself had a tragically short life. Indeed, the femme fatale – having been laid up at New York's Pier 88 in August 1939 – was never to sail again, and instead tragically burned and then capsized at her berth while being converted to a wartime troopship. Her hulk lingered, but then was declared surplus and sold to local New York harbour scrappers and demolished in 1946–47. She was sold in the end for a mere $161,000, her career having lasted for less than twelve years.

The *Queen Mary*, on the other hand, sailed for thirty-one mostly very successful years and today lives on as a museum, hotel and collection of shops and restaurants at Long Beach in southern California. She is the greatest reminder of the grand age of '30s ocean liners. She was one of Cunard's most successful ships and altogether crossed the Atlantic 1,001 times. 'At Cunard, to passengers as well as crew, the *Queen Mary* was just beloved,' reported Everett Viez. 'She had this great, embracing feel – a sort of "magic" not even enjoyed by the *Queen Elizabeth*.' The 1,018ft-long *Mary* was also one of the most valiant troopships of the Second World War. Together with the *Queen Elizabeth*, the two giant troopers carried over 2 million, mostly military, passengers in those wartime years. Quite rightly, Winston Churchill said that two *Queens* helped to win the war in Europe by at least a year.

THIRTIES DREAMBOATS: *NORMANDIE* (1935) AND *QUEEN MARY* (1936) 41

Cut-down and righted, the hull of the 1028ft-long *Normandie* is towed along the Hudson River, to be dry docked for inspection and then laid-up in Brooklyn. (Author's Collection)

42 GREAT PASSENGER SHIPS: 1930–1940

A number of French liners were destroyed by fire in the 1930s including the popular *Paris*, which burned and then capsized at Le Havre in April 1939. (Author's Collection)

Creation of a giant: The hull of Yard Number 536, the future *Queen Mary*, as seen in 1930 at John Brown's yard at Clydebank. (Author's Collection)

Great size: The 80,000grt *Queen Mary* all but overwhelms Trafalgar Square in London. (Cunard Line)

Her Majesty Queen Mary, with King George V to her left, names the *Queen Mary* in September 1934. The event was broadcast by radio throughout the British Empire. (Cunard Line)

THIRTIES DREAMBOATS: *NORMANDIE* (1935) AND *QUEEN MARY* (1936) 43

Preparing for her maiden crossing to New York, the brand-new *Queen Mary* first took a turn in the King George V Graving Dock at Southampton. The *Majestic* and the *Windsor Castle*, both dressed in flags as a greeting to the new Cunarder, are seen on the right. (Author's Collection)

Royal escort: Some 100 craft surrounded the *Queen Mary* when she arrived in New York in June 1936 for the very first time. (Cunard Line)

44   GREAT PASSENGER SHIPS: 1930–1940

Grandeur at sea: The art deco-styled Main Lounge in first class aboard the 2,139-passenger *Queen Mary*. (Cunard Line)

Three decks high, the First Class Dining Room offered as many as 150 items on the nightly menus. (Cunard Line)

High style: A corner of the First Class Smoking Room. (Cunard Line)

THIRTIES DREAMBOATS: *NORMANDIE* (1935) AND *QUEEN MARY* (1936)   45

Captain Robert B. Irving supervised the docking of the giant 1,018ft-long *Queen Mary* but without tugs at New York on 11 October 1938. Requiring skilful handling, the final comment to the situation was that it saved $600 or $50 a tug for Cunard. (Cunard Line)

Seen in a photo dated 14 January 1938, the 59,900grt *Leviathan* has been laid-up at a pier in Hoboken, New Jersey for almost four years. She is soon to depart, however, for shipbreakers in Scotland. (Cronican-Arroyo Collection)

The 1930s were, in many ways, difficult times. The Depression had reduced transatlantic traffic from 1 million in 1930 by 50 per cent to 500,000 in 1935. In this view of New York's Chelsea Piers, six liners are in port together – the *Manhattan* (at the top), then the *Georgic, Majestic, Leviathan, Pennland* and *Paris*. At this time, 11 August 1935, time was running out for the giant *Majestic* and *Leviathan*. Well before their time they were to be decommissioned and laid-up – 'big white elephants,' as one reporter dubbed them. (Author's Collection)

10

SPY SHIP: *BATORY* (1936)

The Polish Transatlantic Shipping Company was organised in 1930 and was the Polish Government's way of creating a national shipping company, especially to New York. It was also part of a project: to develop the port of Gdynia, a former fishing village. Things moved quickly. The new company, using government money, bought the Danish-flag Baltic American Line and its three passenger ships, the 7,800grt *Polonia* and the 6,500grt sisters, *Estonia* and *Lituania*. Gdynia–New York service began almost immediately, including a stop at Copenhagen and westbound calls at Halifax. Immigrants were the primary passengers and created encouraging success. A decision was soon reached to build two 'proper' liners. But with money short in those Depression years, the Polish Government decided on a rather novel payment for the two luxury ships: Poland would provide Italy with a series of coal shipments while the experienced Italians would build the ships. In the process, the company was retitled – becoming the Gdynia-America Line.

The new sisters were constructed by a noted Italian shipbuilder, Cantieri Riuniti dell'Adriatico at Monfalcone. Motor liners, they were designed to make 18 knots at top speed, measured 526ft from stem to stern and were crowned by two rather ornately coloured funnels. Their design much resembled that of an earlier liner, Lloyd Triestino's *Victoria*, also built at Monfalcone. Their accommodation was divided in two classes: 370 in tourist class and 400 in third class. At the time, tourist was the equivalent to cabin class, but being renamed it could be offered at lower fares and therefore appeal to more passengers.

The first of the pair, the *Pilsudski*, sailed from Italy to Gdynia in the summer of 1935 and entered New York service soon thereafter; the second ship, christened *Batory* in honour of the sixteenth-century Polish king, crossed on her maiden voyage in May 1936. The *Batory*'s maiden arrival was, however, greatly eclipsed by the arrival in New York of the spectacular *Queen Mary*. The two Polish liners docked over in Hoboken, at the Eighth Street pier and adjoining the Holland America Line, and were used in the winter off-season for cruises to the West Indies.

Following the Nazi invasion and occupation of Poland in September 1939, the *Pilsudski* was transferred to the British, operated by the Ministry of Transport as a trooper, but had a very short spell in Allied hands. On 26 November, she was torpedoed and sunk by a Nazi U-boat while outside the River Humber.

The *Batory* was much more fortunate. She was laid up in New York following a mutiny by her 300 crew members in September 1939. Caught in a sort of political limbo, she was moored in the Hudson River just north of the George Washington Bridge off Yonkers. A little liner with two smokestacks

The 14,500grt *Batory* is seen during a rare visit to Barcelona, while on a Mediterranean cruise. (Author's Collection)

When she was moved in service to Pakistan and India, in 1951, the 525ft-long Batory was repainted with a light grey hull. She is seen here berthed at Tilbury, London during a summer cruise. (Alex Duncan)

was a strange sight in that part of the famed river. A small caretaker crew looked after the ship for almost a year before it became a fully outfitted Allied troopship. Having given heroic, accident-free service, she was returned to the liberated Poles in 1946, extensively refitted at an Antwerp shipyard and resumed Gdynia–New York sailings in April 1947. Another surviving Polish liner, the smaller, 11,000grt *Sobieski*, returned to commercial service as well, but on the mid-Atlantic route between Italy, France and New York.

The *Batory*'s image was soon tarnished, however. Beginning in May 1949 and lasting through January 1951, she was – in that era of Cold War and the communist threat in the west – the subject of serious incidents. Powerful New York harbour dockers disliked her 'communist ownership' and referred to her as the 'spy ship'. Then, as if to complicate matters, an accused spy escaped from New York and, reportedly with the captain's approval, on a New York–Gdynia crossing. The ship made headline news, but unpleasant news. Now, dockers all but refused to handle the ship, delayed her sailings and workers at New York harbour shipyards – including the Todd shipyard in Hoboken – refused to service her. There was no choice: Gdynia-America cancelled their 1951 sailing schedule and withdrew altogether from the American passenger market.

Quick alternative plans were set in motion. The *Batory* was sent to a shipyard at Hebburn-on-Tyne in England, refitted and restyled – including being given a light grey hull colouring. She was hereafter operated by the renamed Polish Ocean Lines and, in August 1951, began regular sailings on a rather unusual service for a Polish ship: Gdynia and Southampton to Gibraltar, Malta, Aden, Karachi and Bombay. She competed with the established likes of Britain's P&O and Anchor lines, which also serviced India.

48 GREAT PASSENGER SHIPS: 1930–1940

Dressed in flags and waiting in the Lower Bay, the refitted *Batory* makes her first return visit in liner service to New York since 1939. The year is 1949. (Cronican-Arroyo Collection)

In later years, there were annual winter crossings to Boston. The *Batory* relied on general tourists, Poles returning for visits to their homeland and considerable westward immigration. Up until the 1960s, there were no direct air links between Canada and Poland. The ship was in demand. In deep winter, her capacity was reduced to 500 all one class for cruising – from London or Southampton to the Canaries, Madeira, Spain, Portugal, West Africa and longer thirty-day jaunts to the Caribbean. To British cruisers, she catered to an older market, who wanted a more sedate, more traditional ship.

During the 1960s and with prospects still strong and encouraging, it was rumoured that the Poles planned a brand-new liner, a 20,000-tonner said to be named *Polonia*, that would replace the ageing *Batory*. In the end, however, high shipbuilding costs ruled out this project and instead Polish Ocean bought the *Maasdam*, a 15,000-ton Holland America liner. She was refitted and introduced as the *Stefan Batory*, replacing the *Batory* in April 1969.

Within five years, Polish Ocean Lines revived its interest in the North Atlantic, but now to Eastern Canada, to Montreal. In the winter of 1957, the *Batory* ended her Indian sailings, went to a Bremerhaven shipyard and was given a major upgrading. The ship's eight public rooms were rearranged and redecorated, and the twelve lifeboats raised off the decks to create further promenade spaces. The berthing was restyled in more Atlantic fashion – a mere 76 in upper-deck first class and 740 in popular tourist class.

The *Batory* was assigned to a new seasonal service (April–December) between Gdynia, Copenhagen, Southampton and Montreal. There were occasional changes and diversions – to London (instead of Southampton), Le Havre, Bremerhaven, Helsinki and Quebec City (instead of Montreal).

The 33-year-old *Batory* made her final crossing to Canada in December 1968 and then did some farewell cruises. The Polish Ocean Lines decided to preserve her, however. For the price of one zloty (twenty-four being equivalent to one US dollar at the time), the ship was sold to the Municipality of Gdynia for use as a floating hotel. Well intended, it lasted but two years before, in the spring of 1971, she went off to Hong Kong for scrapping.

Dated October 1954, the cover of a log card from the *Britannic*. (Author's Collection)

Artist Bernard Church has done a splendid painting of Union Castle Line's 1935-built *Athlone Castle*. He entitled it 'Queen of the Seas'. (Author's Collection)

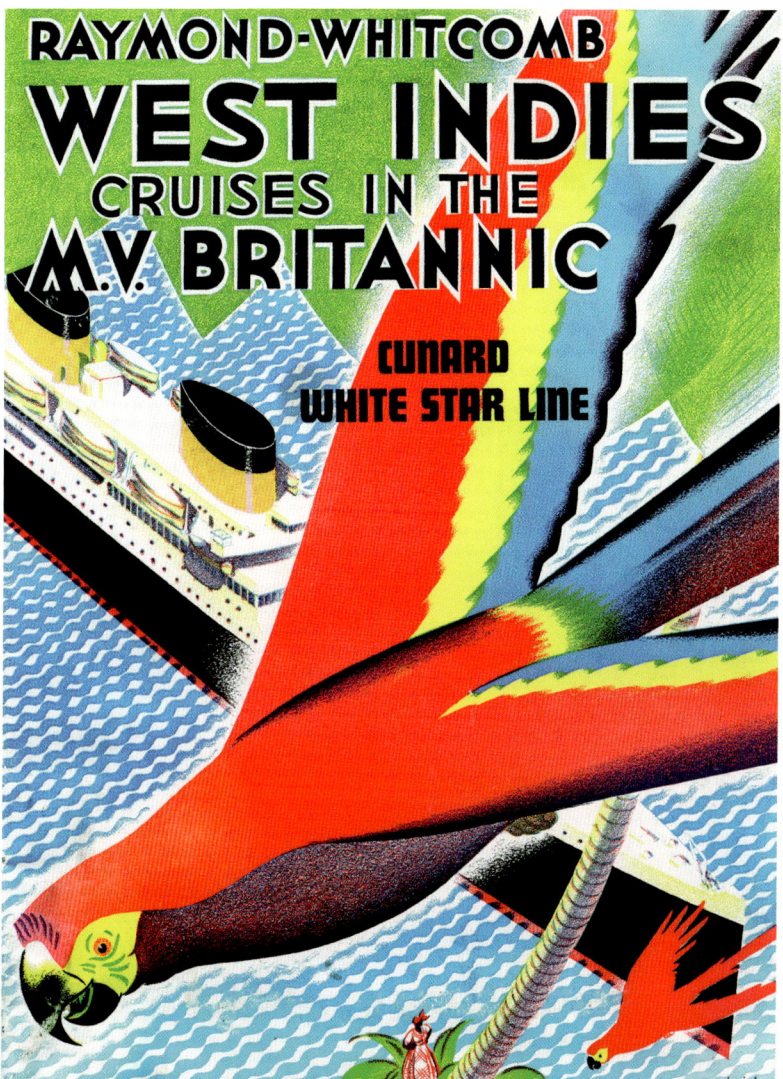

A superb brochure cover from the 1930s. (Andrew Kilk Collection)

Heading down under: promoting one-class, migrant service from the UK to Australia in the 1930s. (Author's Collection)

Poetic nights: a superb poster of service to the East Indies aboard the *Johan van Oldenbarnevelt*. (Author's Collection)

Below: The post-war *Empress of Scotland* on the River Mersey as depicted by the late J.K. Byass. (Author's Collection)

Refitted and seen in the early 1960s, the *Johan van Oldenbarnevelt* passes through the Gatun Locks of the Panama Canal. (Author's Collection)

End of the line: originally the *Monterey*, the *Belophin* laid-up at Tampa in a view dated 5 February 2000. (Peter Knego Collection)

The rebuilt *Hanseatic* with the *Homeric* just beyond at the Steubenhoft at Cuxhaven in Germany. (Author's Collection)

Tropic sailings: a brochure cover for the Miami and Havana sailings of the Clyde Mallory Lines, dated autumn 1939. (Author's Collection)

Artist Donald Stoltenberg's superb depiction of the *Conte di Savoia*. It was created in 1998. (Donald Stoltenberg Collection)

A watercolor by Donald Stoltenberg of a stylised *Rex*, dated 1999. (Donald Stoltenberg Collection)

Fastest ship to the Far East: an evocative post card of the Lloyd Triestino liner *Victoria*, a 13,000-tonner commissioned in 1931. (Author's Collection)

Signalling with her mighty steam whistles, the *Queen of Bermuda* enters Hamilton harbour. (Author's Collection)

Another of Donald Stoltenberg's aerial views – the *Queen of Bermuda* at sea. (Donald Stoltenberg Collection)

Power at sea – the splendid *Normandie* by Donald Stoltenberg from a watercolor dated 1997. (Donald Stoltenberg Collection)

A magical night-time view of the great *Normandie*. (Author's Collection)

Salvaging and righting the *Normandie* in a view from the summer of 1943. (Richard Weiss Collection)

Day at sea: Promenading on the Boat Deck aboard the *Queen Mary*. (Author's Collection)

Artist J. Christopher Butler's wonderful painting of the *Queen Mary*, entitled 'Coronation March'. (RMS Foundation)

The bridge and forward funnel of the *Queen Mary* by Donald Stoltenberg. (Donald Stoltenberg Collection)

A first-class deck plan of the *Queen Mary*. (Andrew Kilk Collection)

R.M.S. "QUEEN MARY"

81 237 TONS

PLAN OF FIRST CLASS ACCOMMODATION

CUNARD

A Cunard poster advertising the coronation of King George VI in London in May 1937. (Cunard Line)

Festivity: Outbound from New York – the *Queen Mary* departs from Pier 90. (Donald Stoltenberg Collection)

The towering three funnels aboard the *Queen Mary*. (Author's Collection)

The *Nieuw Amsterdam* on a visit to Boston in the early 1950s. (Richard Weiss Collection)

Artwork aboard the splendid *Nieuw Amsterdam*: the 'Four Seasons' overlooking the grand foyer. (Vincent Messina Collection)

Artist Stephen Card's evocative depiction of the Ocean Dock at Southampton – the *Nieuw Amsterdam* is on the left, the *Oronsay* is departing and the *Maasdam* is on the right. (Stephen Card Collection)

Artist Bernard Church's sun-filled rendition of another very popular '30s cruise ship, the *Arandora Star* of the Blue Star Line. (Author's Collection)

Artist Colin Ashford's wonderful depiction of the 1930s cruise ship *Atlantis* in the Norwegian fjords. (Author's Collection)

The 80th anniversary of the North German Lloyd. (Author's Collection)

Cruising to the far north, to Spitzbergen, aboard the Hamburg America Line. (Author's Collection)

Christmas cruising: Donald Stoltenberg's depiction of the Hamburg-South America liner *Cap Arcona* at Christmas from a watercolor done in 2003. (Donald Stoltenberg Collection)

Sailing to the sun: a poster depicting Hamburg America Line service to the West Indies & Central America. (Author's Collection)

Shimmering lights: the *Mauretania* at night, during a cruise in 1963. (Richard Faber Collection)

New York harbour in the 1930s with North German Lloyd's *Europa* arriving in port. (Author's Collection)

The world's greatest and grandest liners at Southampton. (National Railway Museum)

```
                INCOMING PASSENGER SHIPS AT NEW YORK
                       August 17th-23rd 1936

Ship      Line      From                          Due         Pier

Monday, August 17th
NORMANDIE, French; Le Havre .................    Noon        88 HR West 48th st
AMERICAN BANKER, US Lines; London ...........    5:00pm      59 HR West 17th st
CAMERONIA, Anchor; Glasgow ..................    8:30am      97 HR West 57th st
PENNSYLVANIA, Panama Pacific; San Francisco..    9:00am      61 HR West 21st st
KUNGSHOLM, Swedish American; Bermuda ........    9:00am      97 HR West 57th st
QUEEN OF BERMUDA, Furness; Bermuda ..........    8:30am      95 HR West 55th st
HAITI, Colombian Mail; Cristobal ............    8:30am      15 ER Peck Slip
ANCON, Panama Steamship; Cristobal ..........    8:30am      65 HR West 25th st
BORINQUEN, Porto Rico; Trujillo City ........    8:00am      27 HR Hubert st
LARA, Red D Line; Curacao ...................    8:00am      Clark st, Bklyn
ACADIA, Eastern Steamship; Halifax ..........    7:30am      18 HR Murray st

Tuesday, August 18th
AQUITANIA, Cunard White Star; Southampton ...    8:30am      90 HR West 50th st
CARINTHIA, Cunard White Star; Liverpool .....    11:00am     54 HR West 14th st
PENNLAND, Red Star; Antwerp .................    9:00am      2nd st, Hoboken
VULCANIA, Cosulich; Trieste .................    8:00am      97 HR West 57th st
ORIZABA, New York & Cuba Mail; Havana .......    11:00am     14 ER Wall st
SAN JUAN, Porto Rico; San Juan ..............    8:00am      15 ER Maiden Lane

Wednesday, August 19th
AIRSHIP HINDENBURG; Frankfurt ...............    pm          Lakehurst, NJ
EXCAMBION, American Export; Beirut ..........    8:00am      Exchange Pl, Jersey C
WESTERN PRINCE, Prince; Buenos Aires ........    1:00pm      43rd st, Brooklyn
ULUA, United Friut; Santa Marta .............    3:00pm      3 HR Morris st

Thursday, August 20th
BREMEN, North German Lloyd; Bremerhaven .....    8:00am      86 HR West 46th st
CONTE DI SAVOIA, Italian; Naples ............    8:00am      60 HR West 20th st
WASHINGTON, United States Lines; Hamburg ....    am          61 HR West 21st st
PILSUDSKI, Gdynia America; Gdynia ...........                6th st Hoboken
ROTTERDAM, Holland America; Rotterdam .......    1:00pm      5th st Hoboken
CHATEAU THIERRY, US Government; Cristobal ...                58th st Brooklyn
FORT TOWNSHEND, Red Cross; Newfoundland .....    8:30am      96 HR West 56th st
MUNARGO, Munson; Havana .....................    8:00am      51 HR West 11th st
MUSA, United Fruit; Porto Cortez ............                3 HR Morris st

Friday, August 21st
CHAMPLAIN, French; Le Havre .................    9:00am      88 HR West 48th st
HAMBURG, Hamburg American; Hamburg ..........                84 HR West 44th st
BRITANNIC, Cunard White Star; Bermuda .......                54 HR West 14th st
DUCHESS OF ATHOLL, Canadian Pacific; Montreal..              60 HR West 20th st
PRINCE HENRY, Canadian National; West Indies..               54 HR West 14th st
ORIENTE, New York & Cuba Mail; Havana .......                14 ER Wall st
AMAPALA, Standard Fruit; Vera Cruz ..........                15 ER Peck Slip

Saturday, August 22nd
MONARCH OF BERMUDA, Furness; Bermuda ........                95 HR West 55th st

Sunday, August 23rd
MAGALLANES, Spanish Line; Vera Cruz .........                42 HR Morton st
QUIRIGUA, United Fruit; Port Limon ..........                3 HR Morris st
```

A list of arrivals at New York in May 1936. (*New York Herald Tribune*)

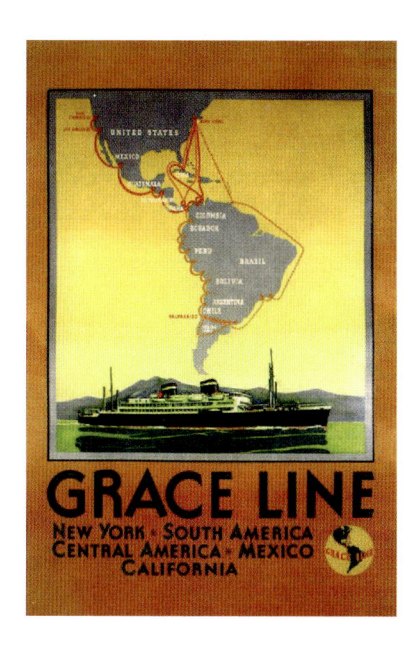

The New York-based Grace Line to the West Indies and South America. (Norman Knebel Collection)

Italia – the 'sunny southern route' to the Mediterranean. (Norman Knebel Collection)

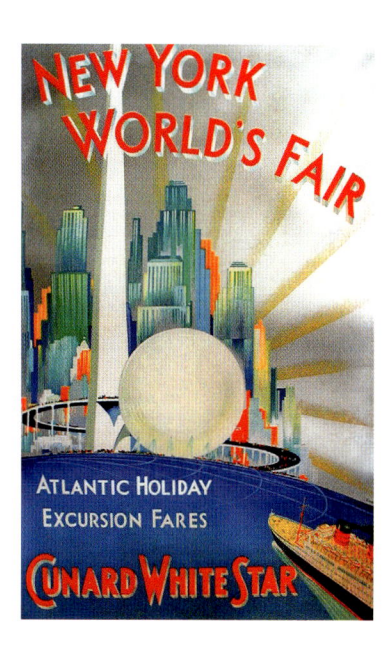

Seeing the 1939 World's Fair at New York aboard Cunard. (Norman Knebel Collection)

White Star cruises to sunny ports. (Norman Knebel Collection)

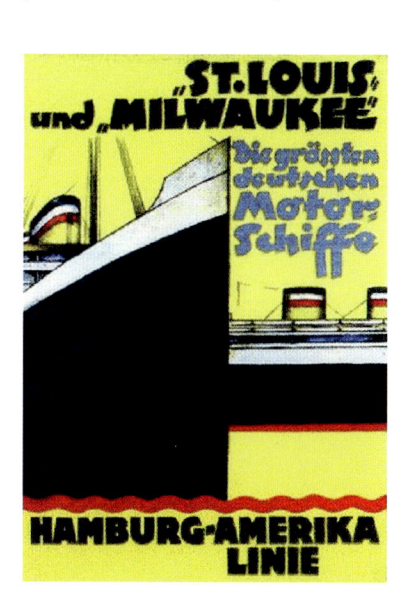

Hapag sisters *Milwaukee* & *St Louis*. (Norman Knebel Collection)

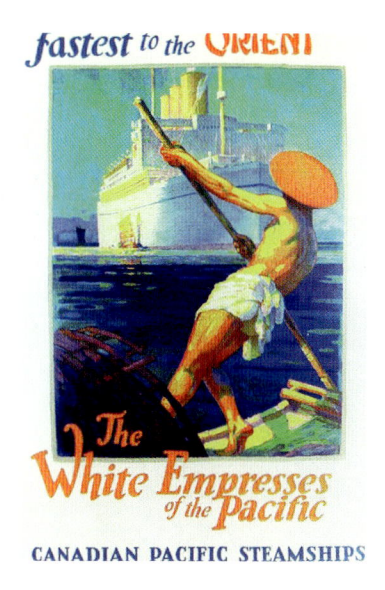

Empress liners to the Orient. (Norman Knebel Collection)

Festive loading & departure scene for the *Bremen* and *Europa*. (Norman Knebel Collection)

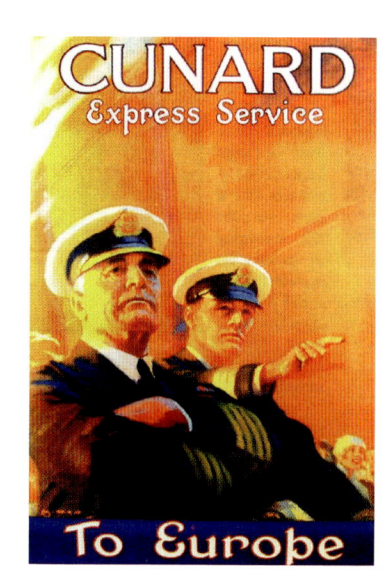

Reassurance: Great seamanship aboard Cunard. (Norman Knebel Collection)

Luxury Liner Row, New York, September 1939 – showing (from left to right) *Île de France, Normandie, Queen Mary, Aquitania* and *Rex*. (Anton Logvinenko)

The superb *Normandie* sailing from New York, 1939. (Anton Logvinenko).

11

AN ENDURING GERMAN: *PRETORIA* (1936)

World geography in the 1930s included vast colonial outposts and links. In shipping, this meant many colonial and colonial-linked companies. One was the German-Africa Line, which maintained an important passenger/cargo service between Hamburg, other North European ports and ports in southern Africa. The company's largest and last liners were ships of the 1930s, the 16,600-ton *Pretoria* and *Windhuk*, a handsome, twin-funnel pair commissioned in 1936–37. Few could have guessed, however, that the former *Pretoria* would endure well into the 1980s. She raised the Indonesian flag in 1962 and was with them until the end.

The *Pretoria* was launched from the Blohm & Voss shipyard at Hamburg on 16 July 1936. She left on her maiden voyage to Africa just in time for Christmas, on 19 December. There was a slight interruption, however. She managed to go aground in Southampton Water – and on Christmas Day, no less. Her passenger accommodation was balanced between 152 in first class and 338 in tourist – in fact relatively few passengers considering her size. She also carried considerable cargo, including fruits coming north to Europe. Her commercial days were rather short-lived, however.

Beginning in September 1939, just as the Nazi war machine exploded fully, she began duty as a military accommodation – and later hospital – ship. Little is known of her exact movements, but she was used for the mass evacuation of the Eastern territories in that decisive winter and spring of 1945. In May, however, she was captured by the British – a prize of war. (Her sister, the *Windhuk*, had been seized in 1941 by the Brazilians after being disguised as the Japanese liner *Santos Maru*. She was promptly sold to the Americans and spent the remainder of the war as the trooper USS *Lejeune*. Laid up and decommissioned in 1948, she never sailed again and was finally scrapped at Portland, Oregon in 1966.)

In British hands, the former *Pretoria* was renamed *Empire Doon* in October 1945, and officially transferred to the British Ministry of Transport, but managed by the Orient Line. The ship was immediately pressed into urgent, post-war trooping. This was to be her work for the remainder of her British-flag career.

In 1948–49, the 577ft-long ship was given a very extensive refit at Southampton. She was even given a new name: *Empire Orwell*. Plagued with mechanical problems, her propulsion machinery was thoroughly overhauled as well. Two of her eight original turbines were removed, reducing her service speed from 18 to 16 knots. Furthermore, she was outfitted internally as one of Britain's biggest and best 'super troopers'. Her accommodation was suitably rearranged and modernised: 359 passengers (officers, their

Sisters together: The 16,662grt *Pretoria* is in the foreground, her sister *Windhuk* behind, in this scene at Hamburg. (Author's Collection)

70 GREAT PASSENGER SHIPS: 1930-1940

Managed by the London-based Orient Line as a peacetime trooper, the *Pretoria* sailed as the *Empire Orwell*. She was fitted to carry passengers as well as troops – 1,600 in all. (P&O)

Awaiting Moslem pilgrim passengers, the *Gunung Djati* is on the left and another ex-German liner, the *Safina-E-Hujjaj*, on the right. The latter had been the *Potsdam*. (Author's Collection)

families, dependents and other personnel) and 1,108 troops. She was painted completely in white, with a thick blue band around her hull and with her twin funnels in the all-buff colour of the Orient Line, who remained her managers. She often sailed out to the Mediterranean and to distant Singapore, Hong Kong and, in the early 1950s, to South Korea.

Years later, Britain began to airlift more and more of her military forces and so slowly began to retire its peacetime troopers. The *Empire Orwell* was first chartered out to Pakistan's Pan Islamic Steamship Company, but it missed out on the opportunity to buy the vessel. Beginning in 1958, her new task was to carry religious pilgrims from Karachi to Jeddah. A year later, she was sold to Liverpool-based Blue Funnel Line, a company known for its large freighter fleet, its passenger/cargo liners and great experience in Eastern waters. The *Empire Orwell* was given another major refit, this time at Glasgow. Renamed *Gunung Djati*, her berthing plan was rearranged again – for 106 first-class passengers and over 2,000 pilgrims. Blue Funnel saw great opportunity arising in newly independent Indonesia and where the Dutch had been expelled. The ship was even renamed in honour of one of the nine great prophets of Islam in Java. Thereafter, sailing mostly between Indonesian ports and Jeddah, she proved highly successful. Chartered by Blue Funnel to Indonesian interests, she was sold outright in three years, when the Indonesian government insisted that Indonesian pilgrims be transported in Indonesian ships. Her new owners were Djakarta-based P.N. Pelni, known as the Pelni Line.

Her official Indonesian owners have actually changed several times, however. In the beginning, in 1962, the Indonesian Government itself was listed as her owner. This changed in 1964 to the P.T. Affan Raya Lines, then to Djakarta Lloyd and finally, in 1966, to the Arafat Line.

In 1973, at the great age of 37, the *Gunung Djati* was seemingly given extended life during a major overhaul at the Hong Kong United Dockyards. Amidst general improvements, she was even fitted with a new set of MAN-type diesels. She even managed to survive a fire at a shipyard pier. There was a subsequent financial problem with the shipyard and resulting in the ship itself being arrested in 1977 at Trincomalee.

In the late 1970s, the ship's pilgrim services ended. Even these passengers took to the airlines. The Indonesian Government awarded the pilgrim contract to Garuda, the national airline. After being laid up for a time at Tanjung Priok, the ship took on yet another new life – this time as an all-grey-painted transport for the Indonesian Navy, becoming the *Kri Tanjung Pandan*. She made a number of trooping voyages between Java, Irain and Timor. In her final years, she was often seen moored at Tanjung Priok. She reached her 50th year in 1986, but was sold (for $250,000) a year later for scrapping in Taiwan.

12

'STRENGTH THROUGH JOY' AND THE WORLD'S FIRST LARGE CRUISE SHIP

In 1990, in what was still West Germany, a rather thick book was released on a most unusual cruise fleet. It was quite an extensive study with extraordinary photographs about an ocean liner service that had little documentation in the West. It existed in the 1930s, certainly an age of high spirits and innovation but also political upheaval and impending disaster. It included two large liners that have been called the 'very first' major cruise ships yet built. This fleet belonged to the so-called 'KdF' – the 'Kraft-durch-Freude-Schiffe'), the Strength through Joy organisation. It was created and controlled by the propaganda division of the otherwise notorious Third Reich. Even Adolf Hitler himself took a keen interest.

The 'Strength through Joy' idea started in 1934 and was a German cruise operation that offered inexpensive holiday voyages to mostly national workers, but in particular members of the Nazi party and their families. The idea was also fuelled by the Great Depression. It was an alternative use for German ocean liners that might otherwise be out of work and idle in those lean times, and which was rapidly losing its place with the important American-Jewish travel market. Rather quickly, it all became very popular and very successful.

German historian Hans Prager wrote:

For an enormously large number of national comrades, a sea journey in one of those big white ships was their first encounter with the sea and sea travel altogether; for the great majority of them, it was also an event which a few years earlier could not even have been thought about. Men and women, who during their life had scarcely traveled beyond the provincial capital, were now seeing the Norwegian fjords, the Bay of Naples, the Canary Islands and remote Spitzbergen.

It had been generally thought that on-board entertainment included political lectures and even Nazi party meetings, but evidently this was not the case. Arnold Kludas, Germany's foremost maritime historian and the author of several dozen books on passenger shipping, added, 'Seventy per cent of the passengers on these cruises were workers and their families. No meetings were held onboard. Perhaps the only intention, the real purpose, was to spread-the-word of the Nazi movement.'

The first ships were recruited from Germany's three major passenger fleets: the North German Lloyd, Hamburg America Line and the Hamburg-South America Line. Always dressed out in colourful signal flags, KdF pennants and Nazi banners, the fleet included such passenger ships as the *Dresden*, *Monte Olivia*, *Der Deutsche*, *Oceana* and the infamous *St Louis*, best remembered

The all-white *Wilhelm Gustloff* docked at the Landing Stage at Hamburg in February 1939. (Author's Collection)

for her June 1939 voyage to Havana with 915 Jewish refugees and later immortalised in both books and a major film – *The Voyage of the Damned*.

The Third Reich could not have been happier with the results. The ships were filled to capacity, the 'applications' for such cruises overwhelming. Within three years, by 1937, orders were placed for two specially designed, quite large passenger liners. Historically, they rank as the first big, all-cruise vessels ever built. The 25,000-ton *Wilhelm Gustloff*, launched at Hamburg, was commissioned in the spring of 1938. Adolf Hitler himself named the ship. While actually owned by the so-called German Workers' Front, her cruising management, operations and staffing were handled by the more experienced Hamburg-South America Line. The slightly larger although otherwise very similar *Robert Ley* followed within a year, in the spring of 1939. She was managed by the Hamburg America Line. As many as eight similar liners were planned, but soon priorities at German shipyards were given over to warships only.

Both the 684ft-long *Wilhelm Gustloff*, as well as the *Robert Ley*, were run purely for passengers and carried no cargo whatsoever. Because of their leisure, all-cruise nature, they were comparatively slow ships, making only 15.5 knots maximum. Otherwise, they were fitted with modern accommodations, extremely sophisticated fire safety systems and two very large searchlights, which were attached to the foremasts and mostly used to floodlight coastal areas for the enjoyment of their passengers. Hans Prager added:

The Main Lounge aboard the 1,465-passenger *Wilhelm Gustloff*. (Author's Collection)

Near sisters together: The *Robert Ley* is on the left, the *Wilhelm Gustloff* behind in this scene at Hamburg. (Author's Collection)

The Smoking Room aboard the 25,484grt *Wilhelm Gustloff*. (Author's Collection)

These ships were, in fact, remarkable vessels in many respects. They became the pacesetters of construction of special cruising, even down to the present day. All 1,465 passengers were allowed to have only outside cabins. And incidentally, the *Wilhelm Gustloff* was the first sea-going ship on which, according to Government instructions, the crew had to be accommodated in exactly the same manner as the passengers.

Unsurprisingly, these ships and the entire 'Strength through Joy' concept disappeared amidst the ruins of the Second World War in Europe. The *Gustloff* as well as the *Robert Ley* were used as Nazi hospital ships at first, but then as floating barracks in occupied Poland. Later, and in an ironic twist of fate, they were destroyed within two months of each other, in the final days of the war, in the winter and spring of 1945.

The *Wilhelm Gustloff* was torpedoed by the Soviets on 30 January 1945, and quickly capsized in the icy Baltic, while assisting in the evacuation of the so-called Eastern Territories (the area around the port of Gdynia), which were then in retreat from the encroaching Soviet armies. Her loss ranks as the worst tragedy in maritime history – some 5,200 refugees, prisoners, inmates from the local concentration camps, wounded soldiers and crew perished. There were no manifests, but some reports suggest the actual figure stands as high as 5,400, even 6,000. This terrible disaster has since been the subject of several books, but – quite surprisingly – had been given comparatively scant attention abroad. Many Westerners still think the *Titanic*, with just over 1,500 casualties, was the worst sea disaster ever.

The *Robert Ley* was bombed out during an Allied air raid on Hamburg, in March 1945. There were subsequent reports that she was to be salvaged and then repaired by the Soviets as the passenger ship *Josef Stalin*. This never came to pass and instead her twisted, fire-ravaged remains were towed to England in 1947 and scrapped.

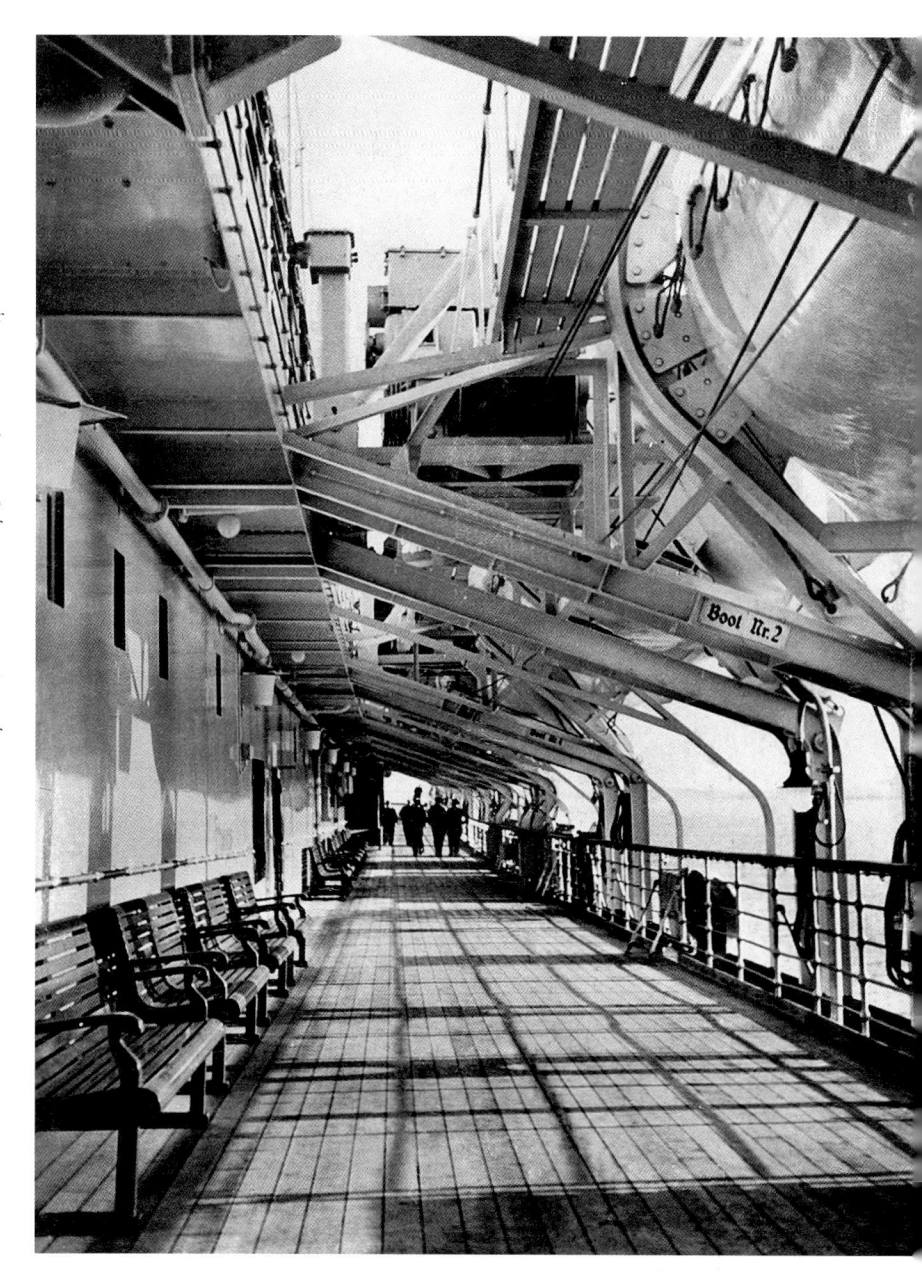

Strolling at sea: The vast Promenade Deck aboard the 684ft-long *Wilhelm Gustloff*. (Author's Collection)

13

DUTCH BEAUTY: *NIEUW AMSTERDAM* (1938)

It was a cold February afternoon, a Sunday in fact, in 1959. The beautiful *Nieuw Amsterdam* was returning from a cruise, from the warm, sunny Caribbean and was arriving at three in the afternoon with 700 passengers aboard. She was due at Fifth Street in Hoboken, not far from my family's home. Among others, we waited for this favourite liner. But tides and perhaps wind were against her and so the liner was delayed slightly – she passed the Fifth Street slip to a position off West 25th Street in Manhattan and then was swung round in reverse position by five Moran tugs. Slowly, she then approached her berth, but approaching it from an unusual northerly direction. Those Moran tugs seemed to work hard in turning the ship and moving her into the rather tight 800ft-long berth. The American Export Lines' freighter *Expeditor* was in the same slip, already berthed at adjoining Pier C. Finally, as the grey-hulled *Nieuw Amsterdam* was all but berthed, the winter wind picked up and the liner seemed to pull away from the berth. Those hefty mooring lines snapped and one suddenly broke altogether, swung off in two halves and then killed a docker waiting at the pier side. The breaking rope, it was said, actually cut the man in two. It was getting dark by the time the *Nieuw Amsterdam* was completely berthed securely on that blustery winter afternoon in Hoboken.

When built, in the late 1930s, the *Nieuw Amsterdam* was dubbed the 'ship of peace' as well as the 'ship of tomorrow'. Regarding the former, she was designed and constructed without a single military ingredient and this despite the increasingly worrisome political situation in Europe. As to her second title, her superb decor was highlighted by some very contemporary, very modern touches, altogether inspired by the Paris World's Fair of 1933 and the upcoming 1939–40 Fair at New York.

After struggling in the early years of the Depression, Holland America had some financial reserves and the guarantee of assistance from the Dutch Government by 1935 to consider building a new flagship – Holland's new 'ship of state'. Her name was to be *Prinsendam* and, unlike almost all previous Holland America liners, she was to be created in home waters – at the Rotterdam Dry Dock Company. Even on the inside, she would be a more contemporary-looking liner – having two well-spaced funnels compared to the rather dated three thin funnels of the previous flagship, the *Statendam* of 1929.

The launching was a happy, celebratory affair. The ship's name was changed to *Nieuw Amsterdam*, honouring the Dutch settlement that became New York City. Her Majesty Queen Wilhelmina officiated in the presence of thousands of officials, workers, their families and invited guests.

Often appraised as one of the most beautiful Atlantic liners of all, the splendid looking, 36,287grt *Nieuw Amsterdam* arrives in New York in October 1948, her post-war return to commercial service. She was routed for nine months of the year between Rotterdam, Le Havre, Southampton and New York (Hoboken); the remaining months were for sunshine cruising to the tropics. (Moran Towing & Transportation Co.)

DUTCH BEAUTY: *NIEUW AMSTERDAM* (1938)

After the war in Europe began in September 1939, Dutch liners – like most other passenger ships – bore neutrality markings along their sides. In this aerial view of Holland America's Hoboken piers, the *Nieuw Amsterdam* is in the centre; the *Veendam* is on top; the *Westernland* in the lower left. (Steamship Historical Society of America)

Crossing the North Atlantic: A dramatic view from the forward mast of the 758ft-long *Nieuw Amsterdam*. (Holland America Line)

It was also a day of precaution: ten large braces welded into the hull and connected to thick chains stopped the 758ft-long ship as she took to the narrow River Maas.

In the wake of the likes of the *Normandie* in 1935 and then the *Queen Mary* a year later, the 36,287grt *Nieuw Amsterdam* had an enthusiastic welcome at New York. She had crossed in eight days from Rotterdam via Boulogne and Southampton, and berthed at Holland America's Fifth Street pier in Hoboken. Praises were high, especially from the press and travel community, and classed her as one of the most beautiful liners of the 1930s. Quickly, she became one of the most popular as well as one of the most profitable.

Commercial life was rather brief, however. After little more than seventeen voyages, she was kept in the safety of New York harbour after war in Europe began in September 1939. In an uncertain period, the *Nieuw Amsterdam* was soon returned to Holland America service, being pressed into alternate cruising to Bermuda, Nassau and the Caribbean. But when Holland was invaded on 10 May 1940, the big liner rushed home to New York, offloaded her passengers and began her conversion to an Allied troopship. Dry docked at the Todd shipyard in Brooklyn and then further outfitted at Halifax, her wartime career began. Within the next six years, she carried 378,361 personnel on voyages that amounted to 530,452 miles (or the equivalent of twenty-one times around the world). These figures represented the astonishing averages of 8,599 persons on each of forty-four voyages of 12,056 miles apiece!

The ship's luxurious interiors remained aboard until later in that year before being all but 'dumped' on a pier side at Singapore. Fortunately, they were eventually shipped to Australia and, then, for safekeeping to San Francisco. They were brought home to Holland after the war ended, in 1946. On board the ship itself, times had changed – comfort and luxury were swept aside. The Grand Hall became a duplex dormitory sleeping 600 servicemen. The theatre held an additional 386. Even the cabins were reconfigured – the twin-bedded suites in first class now held twenty-two officers while first-class doubles slept eighteen.

The *Nieuw Amsterdam*'s wartime itineraries were expectedly very diverse – touching at such ports as Cape Town, Mombasa, Bombay, Aden, Sydney, Wellington, Surabaya, San Francisco, Boston and Liverpool. On a July 1941 voyage, from Suez to Durban, she had special passengers: the Greek royal family heading off to a South African exile. In May 1944, while docked at Hoboken, Princess Juliana, the daughter of Queen Wilhelmina and herself a future queen, attended a morale-building luncheon on board.

It was an especially glorious day when, on 10 April 1946, the war-weary liner returned to her homeport. Coincidentally, it was the 10th anniversary of her launching. All of Rotterdam, or so it seemed, turned out. Crowds cheered, flags waved and horns honked, and one commentator dubbed her 'the Darling of the Dutch'. Her arrival was another symbol of liberation.

Restoring the *Nieuw Amsterdam* was no easy task – alone, it took twelve weeks just to remove the wartime fittings. The actual restoration was stupendous, especially when considering the shortage of manpower as well as materials in post-war Europe. The entire wiring system was replaced as was all of the brass. Some 12,000 square feet of glass was renewed and 2,700 of teak on the outer decks. Some 500 tables and 3,000 chairs restored, and no less than 374 bathrooms were redone with new plumbing fixtures. Within fourteen months, almost working around the clock, the *Nieuw Amsterdam* was readied and restored to her luxurious self. She resumed luxury service to New York in October 1947.

Again, the *Nieuw Amsterdam* was very popular and, in winter, ran cruises to the Caribbean and occasionally longer itineraries to South America. She was succeeded as the Dutch flagship in September 1959 when the brand-new, 38,000-ton *Rotterdam* was introduced. The ageing *Nieuw Amsterdam* had three refits to ensure her continuity. In 1957, she was not only repainted with a grey hull, but given complete air conditioning. Four years later, she was given

The Wilheminakade, Holland America's head office and terminal at Rotterdam: The *Nieuw Amsterdam* is at dock with the combination passenger/cargo liner *Noordam* just behind. (Gillespie-Faber Collection)

Heart surgery: The ageing *Nieuw Amsterdam* gets new boilers in this scene at the Wilton-Fijenoord shipyard at Schiedam in the summer of 1968. (Holland America Line)

DUTCH BEAUTY: *NIEUW AMSTERDAM* (1938) 77

The *Nieuw Amsterdam* (left) and her successor as Holland America flagship, the *Rotterdam*, to the right. They are together, having their annual overhauls, at the Wilton-Fijenoord shipyard. (Holland America Line)

flexibility – from 552 first-class, 426 cabin-class and 209 tourist-class passengers to an adjustable 691 in first class and 583 in tourist class or, according to demand, 301 first class and 972 tourist class. In the summer of 1967, she had something of a 'heart transplant'. After a serious mechanical breakdown (and after which she might have been retired and scrapped), Holland America was able to purchase boilers from the US Navy and have them placed in their 29-year-old liner.

Thought of as the 'spotless fleet', Holland America offered weekly sailings, from April through to October, between New York, Southampton, Le Havre and Rotterdam. The *Nieuw Amsterdam* rotated with the *Rotterdam* and the 1957-built *Statendam*. But in the end, airline competition succeeded – by the late 1960s, the *Nieuw Amsterdam* was running line voyages alone; the two other liners were moved into full-time cruising. By the fall of 1971, Holland America joined a growing group: Atlantic liner companies that were withdrawing from regular transatlantic crossings altogether. By the 1970s, Rotterdam was hosting a new generation of cruise ships, Holland America's headquarters moved to Stamford in Connecticut and even the old headquarters building in Rotterdam was made over as a hotel. Furthermore, the Company liners switched to Dutch West Indian registry and on-board hotel staffs changed to less costly Indonesians. The *Nieuw Amsterdam* had a reprieve, however – she ran cruises to the Caribbean for her final two years.

Complicated by soaring fuel oil prices, the *Nieuw Amsterdam* was not only aged, but highly uneconomic in the end. She was decommissioned in December 1973, and was quickly sold to Taiwanese scrap merchants. Her last voyage was long – from Florida, through the Panama Canal, a stop at Los Angeles and then slowly across the Pacific to Kaohsiung. By March 1974, demolition – those last rites – had begun.

14

CRUISING TO THE SUN: WINTER 1938–39

For me, great fun is a quiet evening or Sunday afternoon pouring over ocean liner memorabilia – looking at those fold-out deck plans, the glossy brochures, the tassel-trimmed menus and, most especially, the sailing schedules. Recently, out of a folder in one of my file cabinet drawers, I found an American Express booklet listing all major cruises from New York for the winter 1938–39. Historically, it would prove to be the final full cruise season for most European-flag liners since, beginning in the following summer, Hitler's forces would slam into Poland and start the Second World War.

Long cruises were very popular in the late 1930s – there were over fifteen listings for voyages of three weeks and longer, from twenty-four to 147 days. There were three trips to South America, three longer ones completely around that continent, two around Africa, four to the Mediterranean and three around-the-world. The then brand-new *Nieuw Amsterdam*, for example, made three trips to South America that winter and topped by a forty-six-day circumnavigation of that southern continent (fares started at $720). Sweden's *Gripsholm* sailed on the same routing, but for fifty-six days, but with a lower minimum fare beginning at $570. There were also South American trips on two of the world's largest and most celebrated ships: the extraordinary *Normandie* and the mighty *Bremen*. For around Africa, Cunard's popular 400-passenger *Carinthia* had an itinerary that lasted seventy-five days and was priced from $680.

To the Mediterranean, there was the magnificent *Conte di Savoia*'s thirty-nine-night cruise ($635 in first class or $400 in tourist), a twenty-five-day run by the French *Champlain* and, longest of all, fifty-six days aboard Italy's *Saturnia* (from $395 in an inside with upper and lower berths in tourist class). And although not counted in the master tally, American Export Lines ran four passenger-cargo ships, the club-like 125-passenger 'Four Aces' – *Excalibur*, *Excambion*, *Exeter* and *Exochorda* – on twice monthly forty-four-day Mediterranean cruises. These were priced from $395 – or $595 with all excursions included.

World cruises were perhaps the most glamorous and certainly the most select. Cunard's *Franconia* took a leisurely 147 days, New York to New York. Her rates began at $1,900. The splendid *Empress of Britain* went for 128 days – $2,300 in minimum cabin space up to $14,000 for a penthouse. With war clouds rising in the Pacific, the Empress's routing was hurriedly changed – substituting Japan with a more southerly detour to Australia. Then there was the yacht-like, 165-passenger *Stella Polaris*, which offered a 111-day global trip for $1,250.

Cruising in the 1930s, especially for the general public, became more and more popular. This evocative deck scene is aboard P&O's *Stratheden*. (P&O)

One of the more popular cruise liners of the early 1930s was Red Star Line's 27,100grt *Belgenland*, but seen here, in 1935, departing from New York as the renamed *Columbia*. (Cronican-Arroyo Collection)

Cruises to the Norwegian fjords and to the North Cape were increasingly popular in the 1930s. Hamburg America Line's *Milwaukee* is anchored in Norway's spectacular Geirangerfjord. (Hapag-Lloyd)

A favorite with the select millionaire set: The yacht-like *Stella Polaris* carried 165 passengers looked after by 165 staff. Often, the 5,200grt ship did long cruises – three- and four-month-long voyages; in summer, she cruised in Northern Europe and the Mediterranean on two- and three-week-long itineraries. (Clipper Line)

80 GREAT PASSENGER SHIPS: 1930–1940

Expectedly, there were many pages in the 'Short Cruise' list. Fifteen days to the Caribbean on Sweden's renowned *Kungsholm* cost $182, nine days aboard the *Oslofjord* could cost $110 and twelve nights on the immaculate *Statendam* went for $152. But even shorter cruises seemed just as popular and especially over the Christmas and New Year's holidays. United States Lines' *Manhattan* had a six-day trip to Havana for $75, seven days to Nassau and Bermuda on the ever-popular *Queen of Bermuda* went for $80 and eight nights to Bermuda, Nassau and Havana on the *Empress of Britain* was posted from $125. Shortest of all was a four-day New Year's trip to Bermuda on Hamburg America Line's *Hamburg*. Minimum was $52.50.

What a collection of cruises! What a collection of liners! What dreams!

One of the highlights of the 1939 winter cruise season from New York was a long cruise around continental South America aboard the giant, 51,656grt German flagship *Bremen*. The 938ft-long liner, seen here in the Panama Canal, then ranked as the largest liner to make a Canal transit. (Roger Scozzafava Collection)

Another popular cruise ship was Hamburg America's *Reliance,* a 19,500grt ship seen here during a summertime cruise from Hamburg to Norway. (Hapag-Lloyd)

Perhaps the most noted cruises of the late 1930s were the four-week cruises from New York of the luxurious *Normandie* to the annual carnival in Rio de Janeiro during the winters of 1938 and 1939. The famed French liner is seen here moored in Rio harbour. (French Line)

15

THE 'SUNSHINE SHIP': *MAURETANIA* (1939)

Such days were quite common at New York in the 1950s and early '60s. There were virtual midday parades of liners, usually outbound along the Hudson and bound for far-off European destinations. I recall one day, in fact, in brilliant summer sunshine, when seven liners appeared within ninety minutes. First, the immaculately all-white *Kungsholm* sailed first, departing at 11.30 a.m. from Pier 97. She was followed by the *New York* of the Greek Line, also sailing at 11.30 but from Pier 88. Throaty whistles echoed throughout the harbour, otherwise busy with freighters, tugs, barges, in fact all sorts of working craft. The giant French *Liberté* followed almost immediately, having also left Pier 88 at 11.30. Representing Cunard, the *Mauretania* followed, yet another 11.30 departure, but from Pier 90. Just after 12 noon, it was the final two departing liners that came downriver – Italian Line's *Vulcania* followed closely by the *Independence*. Both had departed from Pier 84. Then, adding to this 'ocean liner armada,' the Greek *Olympia* was inbound, all but precisely passing the *Liberté* off Hoboken and hurriedly going north to make a 1.00 p.m. arrival and occupy one of the just vacated berths at Pier 88.

In her time, the 35,500grt *Mauretania* was one of the most celebrated liners on the Atlantic shuttle. She had also been a valiant troopship during the Second World War. Miss Billie Ellis was a First Lieutenant in the US Army during the peak years of the Second World War, in 1943. In later years, aboard a current Cunard liner, the *Queen Victoria*, she recalled a voyage in 1943 aboard the *Mauretania*. The ship was then far from her luxurious self, being painted entirely in sombre grey for use as an Allied troopship. She shipped out in January 1943, but far from the 35,000-ton ship's intended run on the Atlantic, between New York and Southampton. The 23-knot Cunard vessel was routed, in top wartime secrecy, from New York. Billie Ellis recalled the voyage as we sat together, some seventy years later, in the comfort of the 90,000-ton, 12-deck *Queen Victoria*'s Lido Restaurant:

> I had been delivered to the *Mauretania* by a US Army tender. The *Mauretania* looked huge to me. Once aboard, she still retained some of her prewar grandeur – the walnut panels that were just magnificent. She was actually stripped down except for the dining room, but there were hints of grandeur. We were a very crowded ship with 9,000 onboard. Even the drained pool was used for sleeping quarters. The officers were given the staterooms while the troops used big, specially created dormitories. There were 6-8 nurses aboard along with 18 doctors. I was assigned to a two-berth room that was now sleeping six, but we still had use of the beautiful bathroom. I remember, however, that the soap would not lather because we only had saltwater.
>
> It was 48 days from San Francisco all the way to Bombay. We made several stops, including Wellington in New Zealand. But no one was allowed ashore. It was all top secret. We were not even told we were headed for India. I was one

The 772ft-long *Mauretania* arriving at New York's Pier 90 on her maiden arrival in June 1939. (Cunard)

of the nurses that helped run the ship's hospital. The hospital was always very busy. There was a rather large hospital in one of the converted public rooms and where there were actual beds instead of cots. There was also a small operating room. We had lots of medical problems. It was so busy that we did not feel the intense heat onboard. After New Zealand, we stopped at Brisbane and then Perth in Australia. We were not in a convoy or have an escort and so it was very frightening at times. At times, it was said that Japanese submarines were trailing us. But we were traveling so fast that the subs, so it was said, could not catch us. The ship vibrated very much. There was no radar back then and, of course, we were blacked out and radio silent. We arrived in Bombay in March.

Three small passenger ships took Billie Ellis to ports along the Persian Gulf, to serve troops suffering mostly from malaria and severe dysentery. She was transported aboard the *Rohna*, which belonged to the British India Line. After three and a half years in the Gulf and in Russia, she herself later contracted malaria and dysentery. She was sent home from Europe by way of the North Atlantic:

> I was sent home on another troopship, the *Hermitage*, which departed from Marseilles. We had many of the American soldiers that had been in the German prison camps. There were often very sick and many were so ill that they died.
>
> We were to sail home to Boston, but were rerouted to New York. As we entered New York Harbor, we stood on deck in full uniform and were moved to tears as we passed the Statue of Liberty. The decks were lined from end to end with troops. Coming home on the *Hermitage* was very, very emotional.

Certainly, the *Mauretania* bore one of its most illustrious names. The 'first' *Mauretania*, a four-stacker that was the undisputed transatlantic speed champion for some twenty-two years, from 1907 until 1929. The newer ship, in fact called the 'new *Mauretania*' as well as the 'second *Mauretania*' for years, was completed just before the start of the Second World War, in June 1939. She barely settled down in service when she was 'called up' to serve as a grey-painted, military-operated troopship. In her new role and travelling all over the world, she could carry 9,000 passengers per voyage, mostly soldiers. She was not returned to Cunard service until April 1947, sailing on a slightly more extended Northern route – from Southampton to New York via Le Havre and Cobh. Her interiors had a warm, inviting, almost club-like quality. Some passengers actually preferred her over the big hotel atmosphere of the *Queen Mary* and *Queen Elizabeth*. The *Mauretania* could accommodate a total of 1,140 passengers – 470 in first class, 370 in cabin class and 300 in tourist.

With over 1,000 passengers and 600 crew aboard, the *Mauretania* carefully docks herself on 5 October 1953. There was a strike of New York harbour tugs. A successful process, the liner was only twenty-five minutes off schedule. (Cronican-Arroyo Collection)

While the 772ft-long *Mauretania* sailed for nine months of the year, she cruised in the off-season – between New York and the Caribbean. Usually routed on two- and three-week itineraries, her ports of call included the likes of Havana, Kingston, Barbados and Cristobal. In 1960, minimum fare for a two-week cruise was $400.

'As crossings declined, she cruised more and more by 1962–63,' recalled John Ferguson, who served aboard and later joined Cunard's shore-side staff in their lower Manhattan offices:

> She was a superb ship in many ways, but those old-style, glossy mahogany-clad lounges had to be made more festive for tropical cruising. The old Cabin Class Smoking Room was turned into the Hideaway Lounge, for example. Cunard had bought cartons of straw hats. We added colored balloons and crêpe paper streamers, which were tacked to the walls and the ceilings. We also added

colored light bulbs. It was a bit like the old hotel trying to be a modern resort, the aging dowager wanting to be stylish and trendy.

Cunard was also trying alternatives. In 1962–63, the *Mauretania* – by then repainted in all green, like the famed *Caronia* – was transferred to an experimental Mediterranean service, sailing between Naples, Genoa, Cannes, Gibraltar and New York. It was an experiment that failed – and failed badly. Again, the ship often had more staff aboard than fare-paying passengers. Afterward, she made more and more cruises, and even took on charters. Any and all revenue was needed: Cunard itself was losing over £5 million a year. The *Mauretania* was used for the opening of a refinery at Milford Haven in Wales and when Her Majesty Queen Elizabeth the Queen Mother opened the new facility she then came aboard the Cunarder for a celebratory luncheon. 'In 1965, the final *Mauretania* crossings were actually charters to the Ford Motor Company,' added John Ferguson. 'They were special, six-day air-sea incentive trips between New York and Lisbon.'

While her Cunard owners perhaps would have liked to see her go on in further service, there were no alternatives, especially for a 26-year-old liner. In fact, only the scrap metal dealers up in Scotland seemed interested. Stripped of some of her finery, the once grand *Mauretania* steamed off to Inverkeithing and was gone within six weeks.

Luxury Liner Row on 5 July 1961 – with (from left to right) the *Independence*, *America*, *United States*, *Olympia*, the aircraft carrier USS *Intrepid*, *Queen Elizabeth* (just docking), *Mauretania* and *Sylvania*. (Flying Camera Inc.)

Above: Wartime service: Painted in military grey, the *Mauretania* waits at New York's Pier 54 in a photo dated 13 March 1940. Two other Cunarders are in port as well – the *Scythia* on the left, the *Samaria* on the right. (Cunard Line)

Right: Twilight times for the *Mauretania*: Painted in green and sent on alternative cruises, the *Mauretania* is seen here in 1965, in her final year of service, at the Ocean Dock, Southampton. The *Queen Mary* is on the left. (Cunard)

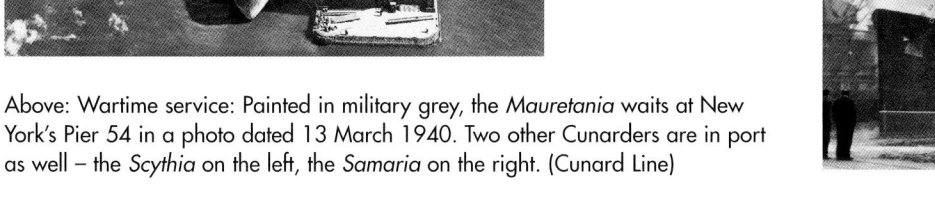

16

LUXURY TO SOUTH AMERICA: *ANDES* (1939)

Unfortunately, she was all but unnoticed. It was high summer, passenger ships were coming and going almost every day and new West German flagship *Bremen* was due on her maiden voyage. Royal Mail Lines' splendid flagship *Andes* had been to New York during the Second World War, but never called as a commercial liner. She arrived quietly on a morning in July 1959, spent two days at Pier 97, at the foot of West 57th Street and then just as quietly sailed off. The 25,000-tonner was visiting on a cruise: a three-week Atlantic cruise from Southampton that included using the ship as a hotel while berthed in Manhattan. I recall seeing her, however, at Pier 97 – and especially with her big gold-coloured funnel rising high above the pier shed's rooftop. She looked very handsome, had a regal stance and appeared to be bigger than I expected and as seen from the pages of, say, a Laurence Dunn book about liners. The *Andes* was not familiar to New Yorkers and not even well known to most American ship buffs.

Britain's Royal Mail Lines, a part of the big Furness Withy Group, was one of the most prominent firms in the South American trade. In the pre-war years, they were especially known for their twin motor liners, the *Asturias* and *Alcantara*, both built in the mid-1920s and acclaimed for their superb accommodations. Highly successful ships, they carried three classes: first, second and – mostly for Portuguese and Spanish migrants – third.

Royal Mail's competitors included not only other British shipping lines, but French, Dutch, German, Spanish and Italian companies as well. Royal Mail's directors in London were especially concerned by the news that France's Compagnie Sud-Atlantique was planning a fast, new and luxurious liner for a South Atlantic service. She would be the 30,500grt *Pasteur* of 1939. Royal Mail certainly had to keep pace with such competition and so went to the Harland & Wolff shipyards at Belfast for their largest and most luxurious liner yet – and new company flagship. Designs were created for the 25,600grt *Andes*. While slightly smaller than her French rival, she was intended to be the finest British-flag liner on the Latin American run. Royal Mail even planned a royal launch for their new ship. Princess Marina, the Duchess of Kent, was to do the honours, in March 1939, but due to sudden political problems in Northern Ireland at the time, such a British royal event had to be cancelled.

Unfortunately, and despite extensive planning, elaborate publicity efforts, accelerated construction schedules and capacity lists of maiden voyage passengers, neither the *Pasteur* nor the *Andes* undertook their maiden voyages,

The handsome *Andes* arriving at Santos in a photo dated 1953. (Author's Collection)

both of which were scheduled for September 1939. Just weeks before their respective departure dates, the Nazis invaded Poland and suddenly thrust almost all of Europe on high alert. While the *Pasteur* was sent to lay up, at Brest, for safety, the *Andes* was still sat at her fitting-out berth at Belfast, but then was quickly refitted as a troop ship. All of her luxurious peacetime fittings were put aside and sent to storage. Her commercial maiden voyage would not come for nearly eight years, until January 1948.

The *Andes* performed heroically throughout the war years, traveling out to the Pacific, the Far East, Middle East and to South Africa. Released and then returned to Royal Mail in 1947, the 669ft-long ship was given over to her Belfast builders and then, with only slight modifications of pre-war plans, fitted-out to her intended luxurious self. Unlike those earlier Royal Mail liners, she would not carry migrants in third class, but instead 324 in exceptional first-class quarters and then 204 in a slightly more moderate second class. She was intended and promoted always for the 'upmarket' trade.

Paired with the older *Alcantara*, which survived until 1958, the *Andes* used her 21-knot service speed to maintain a sixteen-day schedule between Southampton and Buenos Aires with calls en route at Cherbourg, Lisbon, Las Palmas, Rio de Janeiro, Santos and Montevideo. She developed an almost instant popularity and soon had a very devoted, loyal following among travellers – British, Europeans and Latin Americans. Periodically, she was also sent off on all-first-class cruises, to the Mediterranean, West Africa and the Atlantic Isles, and Scandinavia. She also ran a special mini-cruise, in June 1953, to participate in Queen Elizabeth II's Coronation Fleet Review off Spithead. The *Andes* was one of 160 ships present on that glorious occasion, one that will never again be repeated.

When, in the mid-1950s, Royal Mail directors reviewed the future of the South American passenger run, it was decided to build three new combination passenger and cargo liners, with three-class accommodations as well as substantial freight space, particularly for important northbound beef from Argentina. These ships were named *Amazon*, *Aragon* and *Arlanza*. Meanwhile, it was also decided to alter the *Andes* and convert her into a year-round cruise ship. Following her last South American sailing from Southampton, in November 1959, the *Andes* was sent to the De Schelde Shipyards at Flushing in Holland for a two-phase transformation that was interspaced between a 46-day winter cruise to the Caribbean and Florida. When this work was completed and the *Andes* set off on her first official cruise, in June 1960, she was immediately compared to Cunard's *Caronia*, the 34,000-tonner nicknamed the 'millionaires' yacht' because of high-standard, fine accommodation and diverse, year-round cruise schedules. With only 480 berths aboard a large liner,

British style: The cozy Warwick Room aboard the 607-passenger *Andes*. (Royal Mail Lines)

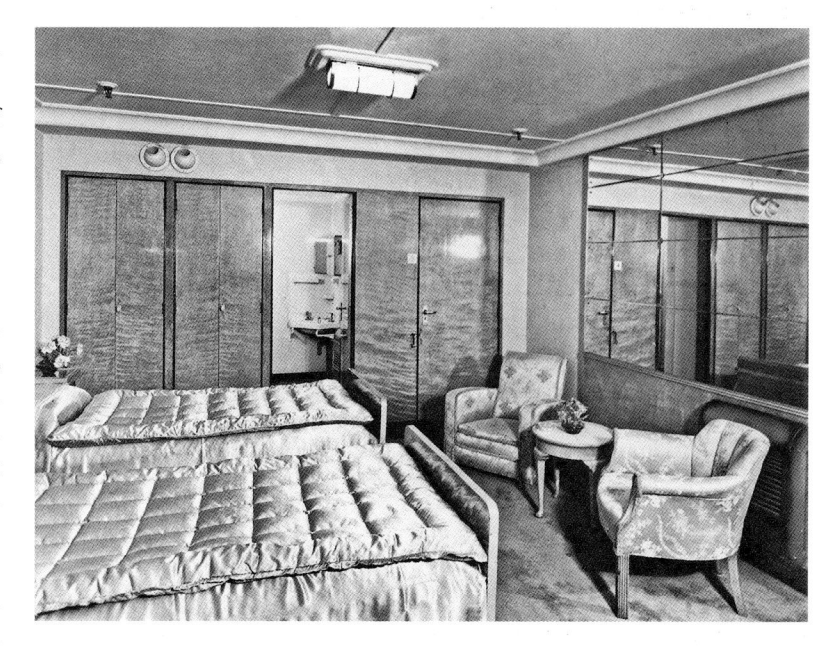

The bedroom of a luxury suite aboard the 25,689grt *Andes*. (Royal Mail Lines)

the now all-white *Andes* seemed even more spacious, in fact being much like a large yacht. This new career, the ship's second life and which would last for over a decade, would bring even greater acclaim and popularity for the ship and her almost bygone era style of sea travel.

New Zealander John Draffin served in the purser's department aboard the *Andes* and recalled her high standards and high popularity:

> She was an exceptionally elegant ship, much like a floating country club. Sailing day from Southampton was like the first day back at school. Almost all of the passengers were 'regulars' and therefore knew one another. Members of the 'Who's Who' of Britain would be aboard. Passengers in the best suites brought along their own servants and traveled with 'mountains' of luggage. There were more crew members than needed, of course, but that was the standard that Royal Mail wanted. There were special considerations and facilities for older passengers. On some voyages, we had more wheelchairs aboard than most hospitals. While we always carried a full dance band, the actual demand was, in fact, for very limited entertainment. There was a very quiet, almost sedate lifestyle onboard. Ironically, in those years, the later '60s, our biggest competitor was the *Reina Del Mar*, a more tourist class-style cruise ship that sailed for Union-Castle, but which was actually owned by Pacific Steam Navigation, a

Summer cruising: During a Northern Cities cruise, the *Andes* – looking like a large, white yacht – is berthed at Hamburg. (Author's Collection)

division of Furness Withy as well. However, while the *Reina Del Mar* catered to corporate Britain, the *Andes* carried aristocratic Britain.

In the late 1960s, Robert Cummins served as a bedroom steward aboard the *Andes*:

> This exceptionally beautiful liner was in the very highest class, possibly more so than some of the famed Cunarders, but with the rather obvious exception of their renowned *Caronia*. The *Andes* was indeed a floating club house, filled with gentry and millionaires and minor royalty, who'd all meet onboard two or three times a year. With 400 or so passengers served by an equal number of staff, we had an almost one-to-one ratio. It was all very English: mid morning bouillon, ritual afternoon tea, formal dinners at one sitting. As stewards, we had to don formal dinner suits and our response to almost any request was either 'Yes, Madame' or 'Yes, Sir'.

In 1967, the *Andes* underwent another two-stage reconditioning and modernisation, in May–June and in December. Even her boilers were re-tubed, which supposedly ensured her lasting through the early 1970s. However, the ageing if still grand ship was facing a dilemma realised by more and more British passenger ship operators: escalating operational costs in the face of declining passenger loads.

John Draffin recalled these final, almost bitter, years, 'The *Andes* was becoming increasingly more expensive to operate, especially after the devastating British Seamen's Strike in the spring of 1966, which lasted six weeks and cost £4 million.' Staffing costs and other demands increased dramatically. Unfortunately, problems for the *Andes* were compounded since she was sailing with fewer and fewer passengers. The old guard was dying off – or becoming too old to travel. Royal Mail brought in some rather brash, flashy entertainment in an effort to recruit new passengers, but instead simply managed to alienate the remaining older, loyalist set. The Furness Withy Group, having just closed down its Furness-Bermuda Line service out of New York, thought of building two new 20,000-ton cruise ships, one of which would replace the *Andes* in the British cruise market. Having all modern facilities and far greater potential for profit, they were to have been quite novel – 'bed and breakfast' ships. The cabin accommodation would be included in the passage fares, but there would be separate charges for the restaurants. Alternately, since it was intended to have such ships in port almost every day, passengers could dine ashore. In the end, however, the managers of Furness Withy and at Royal Mail as well saw container ships and bulk carriers as better investments. To them, the days of traditional, British-flag passenger shipping were over.

Gordon Dalzell was among her passengers in the final years, 'By the late '60s, the *Andes* had passed her best. The pipes were bursting, the air conditioning would break down and there would be plumbing problems. For the most part, however, the passengers remained loyal and accepted these problems and discomforts.'

As the *Andes* grew older and more mechanically troublesome, there was some thought given to converting one of the Amazon-class ships into a cruising replacement. This, too, never left the boardroom. The winter schedule for 1970–71 was to be the last for the venerable *Andes*. Two of her final voyages were among her most diverse: a forty-day sailing that departed from Southampton on 10 January and which travelled to Las Palmas, Luanda, Durban, Cape Town, Dakar and Lisbon; and then, on 20 February, a nostalgic thirty-nine-night cruise to Lisbon, Tenerife, Rio de Janeiro, Recife, Trinidad, Curaçao and Madeira.

As one of a rapidly diminishing group of pre-war luxury liners, the *Andes* was a given a tearful farewell send-off from Southampton that May. With her two masts partially stumped for bridge clearance and in the hands of a small delivery crew, she merely crossed the Channel and then was docked in Ghent in Belgium. She was handed over to local ship-breakers and subsequently broken up. The passenger ship days for both the *Andes* and her owners, the Royal Mail Lines, were finished forever. She was indeed one of the great liners of the 1930s.

17

TENSION AND UNCERTAINTY: THE SUMMER OF 1939

On 31 August 1939, six passenger ships were berthed along New York's 'Luxury Liner Row'. There was the giant *Bremen* on the south side of Pier 86, at the foot of West 46th Street; the ultra-luxurious *Normandie* at Pier 88; the stately, four-funnel *Aquitania* was at Pier 90; and just across, at Pier 92, Italy's all-white *Roma*. Farthest north, at West 55th Street's Pier 95 were two Furness Withy ships, the *Southern Prince* and the *Monarch of Bermuda*. On that same day, but down in Newport News, Virginia, Eleanor Roosevelt – first lady of the United States – named the largest luxury ship yet built in an American shipyard. The 33,500-ton *America* went down the ways without a hitch and was soon moved to a fitting-out berth. But behind the smiles and the cheers of the officials of her owners, the United States Lines, there was considerable concern over her projected transatlantic schedules. Would service to Europe in the summer of 1940 be possible? The political situation in Europe had grown increasingly tense. A day later, on 1 September, Hitler's forces slammed into Poland. Suddenly, it was all over. The lights of Europe seemed to flicker and then went out completely. By 3 September Britain declared war on Nazi Germany. Life for the liners would be changed forever. Amongst that group at the West Side piers, only the *Aquitania* would come back to service at war's end, after 1945.

There have always been rumours that a 'deal' was somehow worked between Berlin, London and Washington. If the *Bremen* was allowed to leave New York (and return to German waters) then the westbound *Queen Mary*, all but overloaded with 2,137 mostly worried passengers and 1,100 crew, would be allowed to safely reach New York harbour. On the evening of the 31 August, with white-jacketed stewards lining the decks and giving the Nazi salute, the *Bremen* slipped away from Pier 86, out into the Hudson and then quietly went to sea. There were no passengers aboard in what would prove to be in fact her very last voyage. Painted over in disguising greys while at sea, she steamed far north to avoid any British encounters. She went as far as Murmansk, then hid along the Norwegian fjords and even flew the Soviet flag for a short time to avoid capture. By December, she was home, moored in Bremerhaven along with her near-sister *Europa*, which was westbound in late August but forced to reverse course once war was declared. In less than two years, however, the 50,000-ton *Bremen* was

Just months before the start of war in Europe, the *Queen Mary* is berthed at Pier 90 and the *Rex* at Pier 92 in this aerial scene dated 24 March 1939. (Author's Collection)

in ruins. Laid up, she was thought to be converted to a huge Nazi aircraft carrier and then later as a large troop transport with huge cuts in her sides to load and offload tanks. The *Bremen* as well as the *Europa* were to be used in Operation Sealion, the Third Reich's intended sea invasion of England. But it all never came to pass and instead the two ships sat unused and largely neglected. On a quiet Sunday afternoon in March 1941, an unhappy cabin steward set fire to the *Bremen*. She was lost. Her remains had to be cut up for scrap and the last pieces deliberately sunk in the lower reaches of the River Weser.

The *Normandie* would never even leave her berth. She sat, quiet and staffed by a scant 110 French skeleton crew, until seized by the US Government just after the attack on Pearl Harbor, in December 1941. But in the hurried, careless conversion to make the 83,000-tonner over as a 15,000-capacity trooper, the renamed USS *Lafayette*, she caught fire and then capsized. She had to be partially scrapped, pumped out and then righted in what was the largest salvage task of its time and the most expensive ($5 million). Her hulk was cut up by Newark, New Jersey scrappers in 1946–47.

The *Aquitania*, soon joined at Pier 90 by the inbound *Queen Mary*, was painted over in greys at the dockside and then went off to heroic trooping. She sailed the world, often carrying up to 10,000 servicemen per trip. She was back in New York in 1945–46 with returning troops, but was soon put on Southampton–Halifax austerity service. Her end – due to pure old age – came in December 1949 when, after almost thirty-six years, she sailed up to Scotland and the breakers. She was the last of the old four-stackers by then, just as the *Queen Mary* would be the last of the three-stackers when she ended service eighteen years later, in 1967.

The *Roma*, which was to be rebuilt by the Italian Line as a more powerful, single-stack, modernised passenger ship, was in fact rebuilt but for Mussolini's navy. The upper passenger decks of the 709ft-long ship came off and in their place went a long flight deck. Controls were based in a starboard side tower. She was even fitted with new high-speed turbines capable of 30 knots. Mussolini's ministers renamed her *Aquila*. But she never sailed again either. She fell into Nazi German hands in the late summer of 1943. On 20 June 1944, the idle vessel was heavily damaged during the Allied air raids on Genoa. She was later sunk deliberately by Italian forces so as to prevent the retreating Nazi forces from sinking her themselves in an attempt to block the harbour entrance at Genoa. Beyond any form of repair, she was salvaged just after the war, in 1946, then cast aside for five years, being moored in La Spezia. In 1951, she was broken up there.

A group of women representing the forty-eight American states heads off for Europe aboard the liner *Manhattan*. The date is April 1939. (Author's Collection)

Rough weather: The mighty *Bremen* encounters stormy seas in this view from a crossing in the winter of 1939. (Cronican-Arroyo Collection)

90   GREAT PASSENGER SHIPS: 1930–1940

Anxious and often worried passengers arrive in the safety of New York harbour on 28 August 1939. Europe will be cast into war within a week and most liner services and schedules disrupted. (Cronican-Arroyo Collection)

The coming war years would be greatly disruptive as well as greatly destructive. Incomplete, Holland America's 134-passenger combination passenger/cargo liner *Westerdam* would be sunk no less than three times before being salvaged, repaired and completed in 1946. (Holland America Line)

The good old days: Robert Ripley, world traveller and creator of *Believe It or Not*, returns to the New York City piers in January 1940. Soon, commercial travel by ship would come to a screeching halt. (Author's Collection)

TENSION AND UNCERTAINTY: THE SUMMER OF 1939

Happy passengers, escaping the war in Europe, reach New York's Pier 61 aboard the little liner *Iroquois*. The date is October 1939. (Author's Collection)

Intended for Europe–South America liner service, the 30,000grt French liner *Pasteur* never had her gala maiden voyage, but was later pressed into service as an Allied troopship. Seen here in June 1940, the 697ft-long ship is berthed at Pier 88, New York – with the *Normandie* and the brand-new *Queen Elizabeth* just behind. (Port Authority of New York & New Jersey)

Painted entirely in grey, the *Queen Mary* is being prepared for urgent war duties at Pier 90. The date is April 1940 and soon the big liner will sail off to trooping service, first in Australia and later on the North Atlantic. (Cunard Line)

Seen on her maiden cruise arriving at San Juan, Puerto Rico, in a photo dated 13 August 1940, the 33,500grt *America* was intended for United States Lines service between New York and Northern Europe. Her schedules were cancelled due to the outbreak of war and so the 723ft-long liner was pressed in temporary cruise service, sailing the still peaceful waters of the Caribbean and through the Panama Canal to California. (Cronican-Arroyo Collection)

18

THE SOUTHAMPTON DOCKS: SEPTEMBER 1939

'Southampton in the 1930s was the most marvelous place to see liners,' recalled John Havers:

> The great number as well as the diversity of ships that called at the Docks seemed almost limitless. Those days were pure delight to the eye and excitement to the soul. On one day in the summer of 1936, I can remember the *Empress of Britain*, *Europa*, *Majestic*, *Montrose*, *Orontes*, *Strathmore*, *Bencruachan* and *Bellerophon* altogether at the Docks. Such collections of ships occurred repeatedly.

A day etched particularly in John Havers's mind was Sunday, 30 July 1939:

> I went out by tender to the *Bremen*. To my complete surprise, she was anchored just opposite Portsmouth, the big British naval base. She was beyond the boom of defense nets, which stretched across from Portsmouth to the Isle of Wight. However, for once, I was quite happy to leave a ship. There were lots of Nazi salutes onboard and 'We Will March Against Britain' songs. It was a very unpleasant atmosphere. I knew then that war was inevitable – even if still a month or so off. The visit really brought home the threatening headlines. As the tender left the *Bremen*, all the crewmen lined the upper decks and gave the Nazi salute. Their message was simple and direct: 'We'll have you later!' To add mystery to the occasion, a strange speedboat encircled the anchored *Bremen*.
>
> Three weeks later, when I visited the *Orcades* on 21st August, I noticed the Docks were full of guns and soldiers. A week or so later, on the 29th, I had my last visit as a civilian. Lamport & Holt's *Voltaire* was already gray-painted and Royal Mail's *Atlantis* as well as Bibby's *Dorsetshire* were in hospital ship colors. This seemed all quite shocking as war had not yet come. The Ocean Dock seemed especially crowded: the *Queen Mary*, *Britannic*, *Lancashire* and the *Arandora Star* were at berth. I also noticed that those long-idle Union Castle ships, the *Gloucester Castle* and *Edinburgh Castle*, had strangely disappeared. For those who watched the docks and ship movements close to perfect accuracy, this all seemed most surprising and very disruptive. A day later, on the 30th, the dock areas were closed to the public. My dock passes were suddenly and abruptly discontinued!

That pleasant tranquillity of the summer of 1939 changed quickly. War was looming – and then declared on 3 September. Like so many of his countrymen, John Havers promptly joined the services in early September:

A very dramatic view of the Southampton Docks with no less than ten liners at dock. Among the biggest liners are the *Empress of Britain*, *Majestic*, *Olympic*, *Berengaria* and (resting in dry dock) *Homeric*. (Author's Collection)

94 GREAT PASSENGER SHIPS: 1930–1940

The 56,500grt *Majestic* takes a turn for refit and repairs in the big floating dock at Southampton. The four funnels of the *Olympic* can be seen in the distance. (Author's Collection)

THE SOUTHAMPTON DOCKS: SEPTEMBER 1939

With one of the famed flying boats in the foreground, the mighty *Empress of Britain* waits at her Southampton berth in the background. (Author's Collection)

I was only nineteen, but because of my ship knowledge, I was immediately commissioned as a sub-lieutenant and taught coding and de-coding. I revisited the Docks for the first time 'in uniform' on 20th September and saw the troopers *Athlone Castle*, *Alcantara*, *Pennland*, *Glenearn* and two 'neutrals' – the American *President Harding* and the Dutch *Colombia* – at berth. A week later, on the 28th, I attended the group sailing of the *Athlone Castle*, *Alcantara*, *Empress of Australia* and *Franconia*. In October, there were 98 ships in Southampton – among them, the *Capetown Castle*, *Orcades*, *Aquitania*, *President Harding*, *Somersetshire*, seventeen cross-Channel steamers and lots of requisitioned yachts. A very rare sight was the little *Acadia* of America's Eastern Steamship Lines. She was running evacuation voyages for Americans heading home to the safety of New York.

At the end of 1939, we heard lots of rumors that the giant, brand-new *Queen Elizabeth* was due, but this was, in fact, 'dis-information'. Instead, she was secretly destined for New York and safety [March 1940].

I shipped out in August 1940 aboard P&O's *Strathnaver*. She was one of the last big ships to leave Southampton. Luftwaffe planes were overhead and photographing us, but somehow we managed to sail onboard in safety.

The great, high-spirited age of the 1930s ended abruptly and, like an opera, with high drama. The stories of the liners of that age continued, of course. Some were tragically destroyed, others changed and still others renewed and revived in the post-war era, after 1945. This book has been another review, hopefully a glorious one, of another golden age in ocean liner history. That photo of the *Bremen*, *Normandie*, *Aquitania* and *Roma* together at New York at the end of August 1939 might serve as something of a conclusion – like an exclamation mark!

BIBLIOGRAPHY

Braynard, Frank O. & Miller, William H., *Picture History of the Cunard Line 1840–1990*

Kludas, Arnold, *Great Passenger Ships of the World Vol II*

Kludas, Arnold, *Great Passenger Ships of the World, Vol III*

Miller, William H., *Going Dutch: The Holland America Line Story*

Miller, William H., *Great British Passenger Ships*

Miller, William H., *Picture History of British Ocean Liners: 1900 to the Present*

Miller, William H., *Picture History of the Cunard Line, 1840–1990*

Miller, William H., *Picture History of the French Line*

Miller, William H., *Picture History of German and Dutch Passenger Ships*

Miller, William H., *Picture History of the Italian Line*

Miller, William H., *Pictorial Encyclopedia of Ocean Liners, 1860–1994*

Miller, William H., *The First Great Ocean Liners in Photographs, 1897–1927*